SPACE
EXPLORATION

Hubble Space
Telescope

Potential damage
of space dust on
shuttle window

Satellite material

Japanese space agency
(NASDA) lapel badge

Toys taken into space

Spacesuit
designed for
use on the Moon

Patch worn by
first Mongolian
in space

Giotto space
probe

McDonald's toys
encouraging youth
interest in space

Residue
from solid
rocket boosters

Vase commemorating
Polish and Soviet
space flight

 EYEWITNESS BOOKS

In-flight
space
clothes
worn
on Mir

SPACE EXPLORATION

Written by
CAROLE STOTT

Photographed by
STEVE GORTON

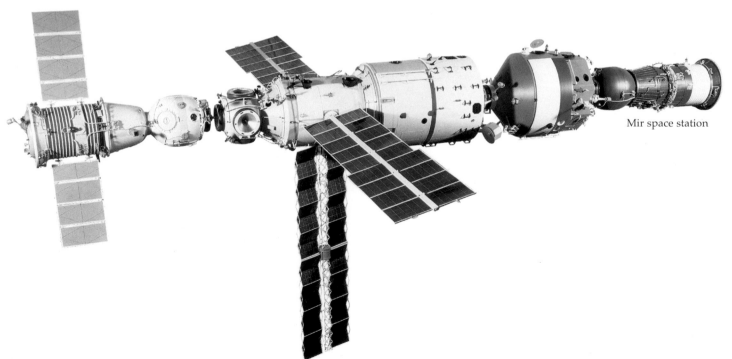

Mir space station

Badge of Soviet
shuttle, Buran

Dorling Kindersley

Cluster experiment
box recovered
from Ariane 5

Astronaut training in harness simulating weightlessness

Dorling Kindersley

LONDON, NEW YORK, DELHI, JOHANNESBURG, MUNICH,
PARIS and SYDNEY

Telstar transmitted first live television via satellite

For a full catalog, visit

 www.dk.com

Project editor Kitty Blount
Art editor Kati Poynor
Editor Julie Ferris
Managing editor Linda Martin
Managing art editor Julia Harris
Production Lisa Moss
Picture research Mo Sheerin
DTP designer Nicky Studdart

This Eyewitness ® Book has been conceived by
Dorling Kindersley Limited and Editions Gallimard

Published in the United States by Dorling Kindersley Publishing, Inc.
375 Hudson Street, New York, NY 10014
4 6 8 10 9 7 5 3

Dorling Kindersley books are available at special discounts for bulk purchases for sales promotions
or premiums. Special editions, including personalized covers, excerpts of existing guides, and
corporate imprints can be created in large quantities for specific needs. For more information,
contact Special Markets Dept., Dorling Kindersley Publishing, Inc., 95 Madison Ave.,
New York, NY 10016; Fax: (800) 600-9098

Library of Congress Cataloging-in-Publication Data
Stott, Carole.
Space exploration / written by Carole Stott.
p. cm. — (Eyewitness Books) Includes index.
Summary: Describes rockets, exploratory vehicles, and other technological aspects of
space exploration, satellites, space stations, and the life and work of astronauts.
1. Astronautics—Juvenile literature. 2. Outer space—Explorations—Juvenile
literature. [1. Astronautics 2. Outer space—Exploration.] I. Title.
TL793.S8 2000 629.4—dc21 97-9546
ISBN 0-7894-5859-4 (pb)   ISBN 0-7894-5858-6 (hc)

Color reproduction by Colourscan, Singapore
Printed in China by Toppan Printing Co. (Shenzhen) Ltd.

Space food: dehydrated fruit

Patch worn by Sigmund Jahn, the first astronaut of the German Democratic Republic

Design for future spacesuit

Ariane 5 rocket

Patch celebrating the first Indian astronaut, Rakesh Sharma

Contents

Dreams of space

Humans have always looked into the sky and wondered about what lies beyond the Earth. For many, curiosity stopped there. Others dreamed of journeying into space, exploring the Moon, landing on Mars, or traveling to the stars. The dream of space travel and exploration turned to reality in the 20th century. The first practical steps were taken at the start of the century as rockets were developed to blast away from Earth. In 1961, the first person reached space. By the end of the century, thousands of spacecraft and hundreds of space travelers had been launched into space. For many, the dream continues. A new generation of space travelers wants to go farther, stay longer, and learn more about space.

WINGED FLIGHT
In Greek mythology, Daedalus made a pair of wings for himself and his son Icarus, in order to escape from a labyrinth. The wings were attached to their bodies with wax. But impetuous Icarus flew too close to the Sun. The wax melted, and he fell to Earth.

GOOSE TRAVEL
The Moon, Earth's closest neighbor, looms large in the sky. Light and dark areas on its surface are clearly visible. Its apparent proximity made it the object of many dream journeys into space. In a 17th-century story, wild geese took 11 days to carry a man to the Moon.

SKY WATCHING
Our present knowledge of space is partly built on observations made by ancient civilizations. Thousands of years ago, basic distances were established and the regular movements of the Sun, Moon, and planets were used for timekeeping and to understand how Earth fitted into the Universe.

FACT MEETS FICTION
As humans learned more about their surroundings in space, the stories of space travel became more realistic. In the late 19th century, the French author Jules Verne wrote stories using scientific fact as well as fantasy. His characters journeyed to the Moon in a shell fired by a giant cannon.

SPACE MONEY
This Moscow statue of a rocket being launched is a mark of the national feeling in Russia for their astronauts and space exploration. In the 1940s and 1950s, research into space travel had been developed by national governments and began to receive serious financial backing. Policies for space travel and exploration and strategies for using space were established.

MUSIC OF SPACE
Space and its contents – the Moon, planets, and stars – have inspired story writers, poets, and musicians. In 1916, Gustav Holst, a Swedish composer, completed an orchestral suite called "The Planets." As the space race was gathering momentum, a young singer (left) named Frank Sinatra was performing love ballads including "Fly Me to the Moon." And the Moon has often been depicted as a magical land in rhymes and stories for children.

TELESCOPE POWER
Until the 17th century, people believed that the Sun, Moon, planets, and stars all revolved around Earth. Observations made by Galileo Galilei, an Italian, through the newly invented telescope showed that space was much bigger and contained more than had been thought, and helped show that humankind was not, after all, at its center.

COMIC CAPERS

The dream of space was at its wildest in the pulp magazines of the 1930s through the 1950s. Authors and artists let their imaginations run riot. Aliens were featured regularly, from encounters in space to landings on Everest. But many other stories were not so far-fetched. They heralded space ventures that were to become reality within decades.

CLUB TOGETHER

Individuals dreaming of space travel came together to form societies. The first was established in Germany in 1927, followed by the U.S. and Great Britain. A leading figure in the British society was Arthur C. Clarke, whose ideas helped to influence space research. His articles and books deal with science fiction as well as science fact. He foresaw the use of satellites for communicating globally and showed us the future of space in his books and articles and also in the innovative film *2001: A Space Odyssey.*

20TH-CENTURY ICON

In 1986, medieval figures that had adorned the roof of England's York Minster Cathedral were destroyed in a fire. They were replaced by figures such as this potent symbol of the 20th century – humankind conquering space. For hundreds of years to come, worshiping Christians will gaze up at this icon of our times.

Earth seen from the Moon

Cratered lunar surface

Astronaut holding American flag

SPACE POP

Space arrived on the scene in the 1960s and 1970s when fashion and pop music showed the influence of the space age. David Bowie (right) took on the persona of spaceman Ziggy Stardust, and his songs "Space Oddity" and "Is There Life on Mars?" echoed the concerns of space scientists.

Exploring the Moon would soon become a reality

SPACE HERO AND HEROINE

Today's children are born into the space age and know that space exploration is a reality. They understand how a satellite works, they know what space is like, and they look forward to exploring it. Even young children's toy hero Action Man (right) and heroine Barbie (above) have apparently both been to space!

What is space?

Surrounding Earth is a blanket of air, its atmosphere. It provides the oxygen we need to stay alive, and it protects us from the heat of the Sun in the day and from the cold, sunless night. Away from Earth's surface, the air thins and its composition and temperature change. It becomes increasingly difficult for a person to survive. The changes continue as the altitude increases and space approaches. The transition from Earth's atmosphere to space is gradual; there is no obvious barrier to cross. Above 1,000 miles (1,600 km) from Earth is considered space, but many of the conditions usually associated with space are experienced by astronauts within a few hundred miles of Earth.

DUSTY DANGER
Space is virtually empty, but anything sent into it has to be shielded against natural or human-made dust specks, which move through space faster than bullets. This test shows how a tiny piece of nylon, traveling at the speed of a space-dust speck, can damage metal.

Nylon missile

Lead with large hole

Stainless steel with smaller hole

Astronaut, inside a craft in a constant state of free fall, feels weightless

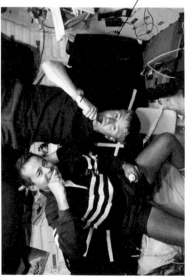

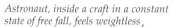

WEIGHTLESSNESS
Astronauts, like these in the space shuttle, can neither see nor feel gravity working on them. But it is there. Their spacecraft is constantly being pulled by Earth's gravity. It resists the pull and stays in orbit by attempting to travel away from its orbit.

Alpha Centauri, which is the third brightest star in the night sky

The plane of the Milky Way Galaxy

ROLLER COASTER
As a car goes over a bump in the road, the passengers' stomachs fall slightly later than their body frames. They momentarily experience weightlessness. A roller-coaster ride has a more dramatic effect, and the feeling can last for a few seconds. Modified aircraft give astronauts the chance to train in weightlessness for up to 20 seconds.

At the top of the steepest rides, it is claimed, passengers are weightless for up to six seconds

LOOKING INTO SPACE

When we look at the night sky, we can see tens of thousands of stars, which, like the Sun, our own star, belong to the Milky Way Galaxy, partly shown here. Beyond are about 100 billion billion stars in other galaxies, which, along with trillions of miles of virtually empty space, make up the rest of the Universe. We have explored space only within the Solar System, made up of the Sun and the planets that orbit around it.

HUMANS IN SPACE

Most astronauts, like these, have traveled into space close to Earth, where they use the planet's gravity to orbit around it. Only 26 have traveled farther, to the Moon. Wherever humans go in space, they need to take their own atmosphere and protection against the new environment.

Suits protect astronauts from temperatures ranging from 250°F (121°C) to -150°F (-101°C)

Rock from Mars fell to Earth about 13,000 years ago

Voyager spacecraft is prepared for launch in 1977

DOWN TO EARTH

Scientists get to study a piece of space material by sending robotic craft or astronauts to investigate it on site or bring it back to Earth. They also study chunks that have found their own way here. Every year, over 3,000 bits of space rock fall to Earth. Most fall into the sea, but a handful are collected.

MESSAGE FROM EARTH

It is believed that one in every 25 stars has planets. The Sun's nine are the only confirmed planets. Of these, Earth is the only one known to have life. However, some spacecraft, such as Voyager, carry messages in case intelligent life exists elsewhere and finds them.

Disk with message

HIGH-ALTITUDE EXPLORERS

There is no need to leave Earth to experience a change in altitude and a consequent change in Earth's atmosphere. Mountaineers know that the air gets thinner the higher they climb. At about 12,000 ft (3,600 m), there is less oxygen, and they need to carry their own. High-altitude balloonists travel in pressurized cabins. At 12 miles (19.30 km) above sea level, atmospheric pressure is so low that body fluids vaporize and force their way through openings, such as eyes and ears.

Earth's highest mountain, Everest, is 29,029 ft (8,848 m) above sea level

Space nations

PEOPLE FROM AROUND THE WORLD are involved in space exploration. The vast majority will never go anywhere near space, but it is a major part of their lives. Only a handful of the world's nations are capable of launching vehicles into space, but many more countries are involved in the preparation and manufacture of spacecraft and technology. Others are involved in monitoring space activities. All are reaping the benefits of space exploration – from the knowledge they gain of the Universe to the cheap and instant telephone calls they make via satellites. Some nations work alone, others pool financial resources, knowledge, and expertise. Sending an astronaut, a space probe, or a satellite into space is a billion-dollar venture accomplished by thousands of people and benefiting millions more.

MISSION BADGE
Each flight carrying astronauts or launching space probes has its own cloth badge. It features a selection of pictures and words representing the mission. France was the first nation to have astronauts fly aboard both Soviet and American spacecraft. Jean-Loup Chrétien's stay aboard Salyut 7 in 1982 was marked by this commemorative badge.

Engine nozzle

Thruster rockets for fine control

APOLLO 18
America's Apollo 18 completed the first international space rendezvous when it maneuvered toward the Soviets' Soyuz 19 in 1975. It carried the docking adapter to join the two craft.

GETTING THERE
Metals and parts used in spacecraft are produced by many manufacturers and are brought together for assembly and testing. The completed craft is then transported to the launch site. A large piece of space equipment, such as this major part of the Ariane 5 rocket, is transported by water. Here, it is being pulled through a harbor en route to its launch site at Kourou in French Guiana, South America.

КОСМОС ДЛЯ МИРА
COSMOS FOR PEACE

MISSION CONTROL, CHINA
China sent its first satellite, Mao 1, into space in 1970. Since 1986, China has been a commercial launcher of satellites for other nations. This picture shows mission control staff at the Xichang site practicing launch procedure.

SOUNDS OF SPACE
Space exploration has inspired people around the world to paint, write, and compose. This two-record set was released in 1975 at the time of the Apollo-Soyuz docking as a celebration of Soviet space achievement. One record includes space-to-ground transmission. The second plays patriotic songs. One song is sung by Yuri Gagarin, who was the first man ever to go into space.

Giant dish provides telephone and television links

THE EARS OF THE WORLD

Ground stations around the world are listening to space. Giant dishes collect data transmitted by distant planetary probes, by satellite observatories looking into space and monitoring Earth, and by communication satellites providing telephone links and television pictures. This 39 ft 4 in (12 m) dish at Lhasa in Tibet is used for telecommunications.

INDIA IN SPACE

India launched its first satellite in 1980, becoming the seventh nation to launch a space rocket. This badge marks the flight of Indian astronaut Rakesh Sharma to the Salyut 7 space station in April 1984.

HEADLINE NEWS

Sending astronauts into space has become such a regular event that it is reported on the inside pages of a newspaper, if at all. But when a country's first astronaut is launched, it makes headline news. The flight of the first astronaut from Poland, Miroslaw Hermaszewski in 1978, and of the first Cuban, Arnaldo Tamayo Mendez in 1980, were celebrated in their national press.

Docking adapter

SOYUZ 19

Soyuz 19 was launched first, from the Soviet Union. A few hours later, Apollo 18 took off. During docking, Soyuz kept pointing at Apollo and rolled to match its movement.

Aleksei Leonov (center) with Americans Thomas Stafford and Donald Slayton

INTERNATIONAL RENDEZVOUS

In 1975, Americans and Russians linked up for the first time in space. Three American astronauts aboard Apollo 18 and two Russians on Soyuz 19 flew in tandem as they orbited the world. Once docked on July 17, they stayed together for two days. The crew moved between the two craft, and they worked and ate together. In the 1990s, the American space shuttle started regular trips to Mir, where the two nations work together.

WELCOME GIFT

International space crews exchange gifts. Russians sometimes give candies like these. Space crews aboard Mir greet visiting astronauts with a traditional Russian gift of bread and salt as the visitors enter the space station. On Earth, the white floury bread is broken and eaten after dipping it in coarse salt. The food has been adapted into prepackaged bread and salt wafers for space travel.

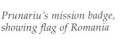

Prunariu's mission badge, showing flag of Romania

Gurragcha's mission badge, showing flag of Mongolia

ROMANIA IN SPACE

Dumitru Prunariu was the first Romanian to enter space when he flew on Soyuz 40 to the Salyut 6 space station in May 1981. Along with fellow astronaut Russian Leonid Popov, Prunariu underwent psychological and medical tests. The custom of photographing the visiting astronaut's country was carried out as the station passed over Romania in daylight.

SEARCHING MONGOLIA

The eighth international crew on board a Soviet space station included Mongolian astronaut Jugderdemidiyn Gurragcha, who was on board Salyut 6 for eight days in March 1981. He carried out a number of experiments. Using mapping and other cameras, he searched for possible ore and petroleum deposits in Mongolia.

Rocket science

A ROCKET IS NEEDED to get anything and anyone into space. It provides the power to lift itself and its cargo off the ground and, in a short span of time, the power to attain the speed that will carry it away from gravity's pull and into space. The burning rocket fuels produce hot gases that are expelled through an exhaust nozzle at the bottom of the rocket. This provides the force that lifts the vehicle off the ground. The space rocket was developed in the first half of the 20th century. Typically, two rockets a week are launched into space from somewhere in the world.

EARLY ROCKETS
The earliest rockets were used by the Chinese about 1,000 years ago. They were powered with gunpowder. When ignited, an explosive burst propelled the rocket forward. They resembled fireworks but were used as weapons. This 17th-century man shot rocket arrows from a basket.

ROCKET PIONEER
Konstantin Tsiolkovsky, a Russian, started working on the theory of rocket space flight in the 1880s. He worked out how fast a rocket needed to go and how much fuel it would require. He proposed using liquid fuel and igniting it in several stages.

ROCKET ENGINE
This is one of the four Viking engines that powered the Ariane 1 rocket. It is an unusual view: looking up into it from below as it stands on the launch pad. In under 2.5 minutes, at 31 miles (50 km) above ground, its job was over.

Honeycomb material is light and strong

Giant Viking rocket engine

Honeycomb structure is visible from the top

MADE TO MEASURE
The materials used in rockets and their cargoes need to be light. A lighter rocket needs less fuel to launch it, and so it is less costly. The materials also need to be strong and able to withstand the thrust at launch. Some widely available substances, such as steel are used. Others, like this honeycomb material, are specially developed by rocket scientists and manufactured by space engineers.

Nozzle where gases, produced by burning fuel in booster rocket, are expelled

Pipe delivers oxygen to hydrogen for combustion

Flags of nations involved in Ariane 5 project

25 tons of liquid hydrogen are stored in tank placed here

Solid rocket boosters supply 90 percent of thrust at liftoff

130 tons of liquid oxygen are stored in a separate tank

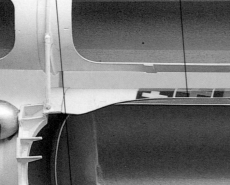

Combustion chamber where the fuel and oxidizer are mixed and burn

Helium tank

Liftoff procedure starts with the ignition of this Vulcain engine

French Space Agency emblem

Two boosters supply initial thrust before main rocket is ignited

European Space Agency (ESA) emblem

French rocket-manufacturing company (Arianespace) emblem

ROCKET CAR

Fuel for use in rockets was tested in cars, rail vehicles, air gliders, and ice sledges in the 1920s. The cars resembled a rocket in shape and in the noise they made as they burned the fuel. They either used liquid fuel or powdered solid fuel. The men who built and drove the cars were members of the newly formed German Society for Space Travel.

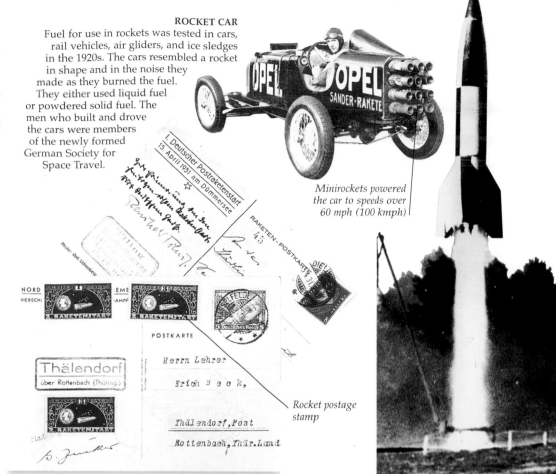

Minirockets powered the car to speeds over 60 mph (100 kmph)

LIQUID-FUEL ROCKET

American Robert Goddard was fascinated by the idea of space travel. He experimented with rockets and different fuels. He launched the first-ever liquid-fuel rocket in 1926. The flight lasted 2.5 seconds and the rocket reached an altitude of 40 ft (12.5 m).

ROCKET MAIL

Enterprising ways of using rocket power were developed in the 1930s. These cards were sent across Germany by rocket mail in 1931. They were specially produced cards, using special rocket postage stamps. Ventures such as this were short-lived.

Rocket postage stamp

ISLAND TO SPACE

Japan's Tanegashima space center is one of over 20 launch sites around the world where rockets start their space journeys. From this island site, the Japanese space agency assembles, tests, launches, and keeps track of satellites. Japan became the fourth nation into space when it launched its first satellite in 1970. Launch sites are built close to Earth's equator to benefit from an extra push at launch from the Earth's spin.

FIRST TO SPACE

The V-2 rocket was developed in Germany in the 1930s. Its first successful launch was in 1942, and it became the first mass-produced long-range rocket. It was first used as a weapon. Over 1,000 were fired at Great Britain in the last year of World War II. After the war, the V-2 and subsequent rockets for space travel were developed by an American team headed by a German, Wernher von Braun.

Parachute in nose cone for slow descent

Engine and fuel will move the pair of satellites into the correct orbit

Up to four satellites, like this one, can be carried into space

ARIANE 5

This Ariane rocket is the launch vehicle of the European Space Agency (ESA). The agency is made up of 14 European countries that fund and develop satellites and experiments for space. Over 120 satellites have been launched by Ariane rockets from the ESA launch site at Kourou in French Guiana. The latest of the Ariane series, Ariane 5 is the most powerful. It is therefore able to launch heavy single satellites or a few smaller ones. It has also been designed to allow astronauts to be transported in a specially modified upper stage.

Reusable rocket

PIGGYBACK RIDE
When a shuttle orbiter (space plane) needs to be moved to a launch site, it is transported piggyback style on top of a specially adapted Boeing 747 aircraft. The shuttle is then prepared for launch and is fitted with boosters and a fuel tank for takeoff.

WHEN THE FIRST SPACE SHUTTLE was launched in 1981, it marked a turning point in space travel. Conventional one-use rockets had until then been the only way of sending astronauts or cargoes to space. If space travel was to become a regular event, a reusable system was needed. The United States came up with the answer in the form of the Space Transportation System (STS), or space shuttle, for short. It is launched like a conventional rocket but returns to Earth like a plane. This means that two of its three main parts can be used over and over again. Shuttles are now used for launching, retrieving, and repairing satellites and launching space probes, and also as space laboratories where astronauts work on experiments.

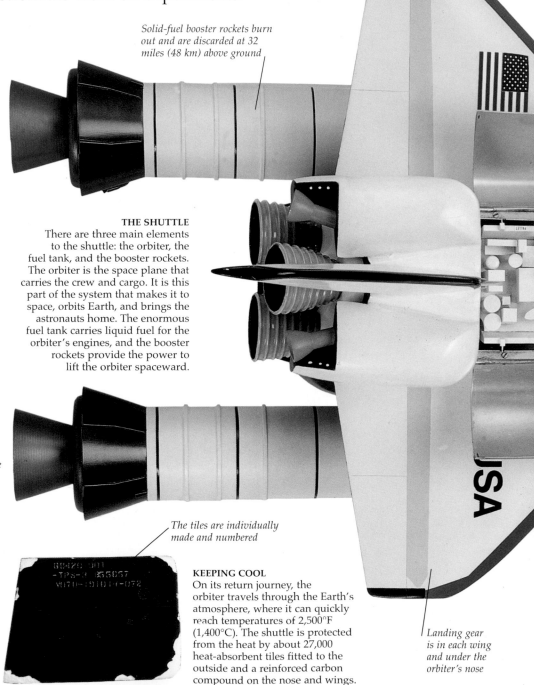

Solid-fuel booster rockets burn out and are discarded at 32 miles (48 km) above ground

THE SHUTTLE
There are three main elements to the shuttle: the orbiter, the fuel tank, and the booster rockets. The orbiter is the space plane that carries the crew and cargo. It is this part of the system that makes it to space, orbits Earth, and brings the astronauts home. The enormous fuel tank carries liquid fuel for the orbiter's engines, and the booster rockets provide the power to lift the orbiter spaceward.

BLASTOFF
Within two minutes of the shuttle's liftoff from the launch pad, the booster rockets are discarded, as is the fuel tank six minutes later. From liftoff to space takes less than ten minutes. Since the first launch in 1981, there have been over 80 successful flights. Atlantis's launch in October 1985, shown here, was the 21st shuttle mission.

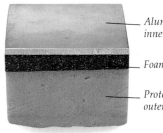

Aluminum inner structure

Foam coating

Protective outer layer

SAFE INSIDE
The shuttle's aluminum fuel tank is higher than a 15-story building. It has been specially designed to carry and protect its cargo. Inside its outer layer, shown here, are two pressurized tanks that contain liquid hydrogen and liquid oxygen. During launch, the fuel is fed to the orbiter's three main engines.

The tiles are individually made and numbered

KEEPING COOL
On its return journey, the orbiter travels through the Earth's atmosphere, where it can quickly reach temperatures of 2,500°F (1,400°C). The shuttle is protected from the heat by about 27,000 heat-absorbent tiles fitted to the outside and a reinforced carbon compound on the nose and wings.

Landing gear is in each wing and under the orbiter's nose

SOVIET SHUTTLE
Other countries have researched and developed the principle of reusable space transport, but November 1988 saw the only launch that came close, that of the Soviet shuttle Buran. The crewless shuttle flew two orbits of the Earth and returned by automatic landing.

HYPERSONIC AIRCRAFT
During the 1960s, the X-15 rocket-powered aircraft was used to investigate flight at hypersonic speeds. It was released at high altitude, where the rocket motors were ignited. The pilot controlled the X-15 at about 4,000 mph (6,500 kmph). Experience gained with this craft was used in the design of the shuttle.

On board is Sally Ride, the first American female astronaut

SHUTTLE ASTRONAUTS
Each shuttle has a commander responsible for the whole flight, a pilot who flies the orbiter, and a number of astronaut specialists. Mission specialists are in charge of the orbiter's systems and perform spacewalks. Payload specialists, who may or may not be regular astronauts, work with particular equipment or experiments on board.

ORBITER IN FLIGHT
The U.S. developed five orbiters for its shuttle fleet – Columbia, Discovery, Atlantis, Challenger and Endeavour. The orbiter Challenger is shown here on its second flight, in June 1983. Challenger flew nine times before exploding just after liftoff in 1986.

John Young, commander, (left) and Robert Crippen, pilot, in training for the first ever shuttle flight

Payload bay doors open in flight

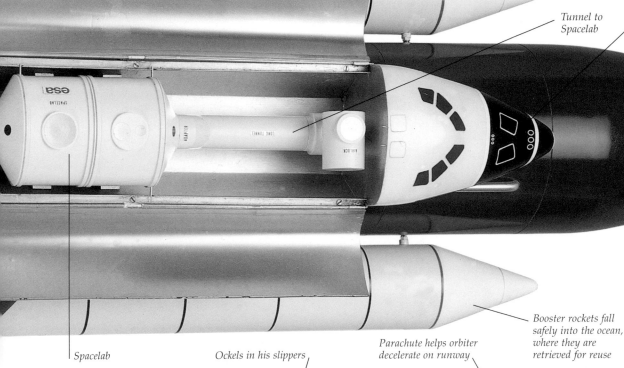

Tunnel to Spacelab

Flight deck and crew quarters for up to eight astronauts

External fuel tank is emptied in the first eight and a half minutes of flight. It is discarded and breaks up in the atmosphere

Spacelab

Ockels in his slippers

Parachute helps orbiter decelerate on runway

Booster rockets fall safely into the ocean, where they are retrieved for reuse

INSIDE SPACELAB
Wubbo Ockels, Dutch astronaut, was a payload specialist on Challenger's third mission, in 1985. He worked inside Spacelab during the seven-day flight. There were 75 experiments on board, several of which were designed to give scientists data on how space travel affects the human body (pp. 28–29).

SHUTTLE LANDING
An orbiter's on-board motors are used to maneuver in space and position the craft to come out of orbit and decelerate. The orbiter enters the atmosphere at 15,000 mph (24,000 kmph), slowing all the time. A loss of communications then follows for 12–16 minutes. Then the orbiter touches down on the runway at 214 mph (344 kmph), coming to rest after 1.5 miles (2.4 km).

The race for space

TWO NATIONS DOMINATED one of the most intense and successful periods of space exploration. For around 15 years, centered on the 1960s, America and the Soviet Union raced against each other to achieve success in space. Each wanted to make notable firsts: to be the first to put a satellite, and then a man, into space; to have the first astronaut in orbit and the first woman space traveler; to take the first spacewalk outside a craft; and to be the first to step onto the Moon. The race got under way when the Soviets launched Sputnik 1, proving their space capability to the surprised Americans. From then on, each leaped forward in turn as new space achievements were made one after another.

UNITED CIGARETTES
These cigarettes celebrate the docking of the American Apollo 18 and Soviet Soyuz 19 in space in July 1975.

Apollo-Soyuz union cigarettes were printed in American on one side and Russian on the other

Aluminum sphere 1 ft 11 in (58 cm) across with four antennas

SPUTNIK 1
The space age started on October 4, 1957, when the first artificial satellite was launched by the Soviets. The satellite helped scientists learn more about the nature of Earth's uppermost atmosphere. As it orbited Earth every 96 minutes, its two radio transmitters signaled "bleep bleep."

EXPLORER 1
The rocket that was to carry the first American satellite into space, Vanguard, exploded on the launch pad. However, satellite, Explorer 1, was already being constructed and, on January 31, 1958, it became the first American satellite in space. The Van Allen radiation belts surrounding Earth were discovered using scientific equipment on board.

Explorer 1 orbited Earth for 12 years

Service module was jettisoned before re-entry into Earth's atmosphere

Electrodes were attached to Laika to monitor her heart and breathing

Luna 9 transmitted panoramic views of the lunar surface back to Earth

LUNA 9
In 1959, the first of the Luna series of craft was launched by the Soviets. Luna 1 was the first spacecraft to leave Earth's gravity. Luna 9 was the first craft to make a successful landing on the Moon. The Soviets also sent the first of their Venera series to Venus in 1961.

LAIKA, THE FIRST CREATURE IN SPACE
Only one month after the launch of Sputnik 1, the Soviets launched the first living creature into space aboard Sputnik 2. A dog called Laika traveled in a padded pressurized compartment and survived for a few days. The satellite was much heavier than anything the Americans were planning and suggested the Soviets were considering putting humans in orbit. American pride was injured, and space became a political issue. The Americans resolved to enter and win the race.

APOLLO 11
In the early 1960s, 377,000 Americans worked to get a man on the Moon. Ten two-man Gemini missions showed that the Americans could successfully spacewalk, spend time in space, and dock craft. These were all necessary for the three-man Apollo program, the one that would take men to the Moon (pp. 22–23).

FIRST AMONG EQUALS
Yuri Gagarin became the first human in space on April 12, 1961. Strapped in his Vostok 1 capsule, he orbited Earth once, spending 108 minutes in space. After re-entering Earth's atmosphere, he ejected himself from the capsule and parachuted to Earth. With him here is Valentina Tereshkova, the first woman in space.

HERO'S WELCOME
Gagarin's countrymen turned out in force to welcome him home from space. They filled the enormous Red Square in the heart of Moscow. But Gagarin was not only a hero in the Soviet Union. In the months ahead, crowds turned out to greet him wherever he toured.

Three-man crew worked and slept in the command module, the only part of the craft to return to Earth

A PRESIDENT'S PROMISE
In the late 1950s, America increased space research funding and formed a space agency, NASA (National Aeronautics and Space Administration). Its first goal was to place a man in space. The Soviets beat them to it by one month. But in May 1961 America's new president, John F. Kennedy, set a new goal of "landing a man on the Moon and returning him safely to the Earth" before the decade was out.

FIRST SPACEWALK
Once humans had successfully flown into space, both the Soviets and the Americans prepared to let them move outside their craft in space. The first EVA (Extravehicular Activity), or spacewalk, was made by Soviet cosmonaut Aleksei Leonov in March 1965. He wore his specially designed suit throughout the mission.

Command and service modules where crew is located

LIFTOFF
The Saturn V rocket was developed to launch the Apollo craft to the Moon. As tall as a 33-story building, it was the most powerful rocket to date. The majority of its bulk was fuel. The top third of the rocket consisted of: the lunar module for landing on the Moon; the service module, providing the oxygen, water, and power for the crew; and, right on top, the command module.

THE MOON TO MEXICO
Michael Collins (left), Buzz Aldrin (rear), and Neil Armstrong of Apollo 11, the first mission to land men on the Moon, are greeted in Mexico City. The three visited 24 countries in 45 days as part of a goodwill tour after their safe return from the Moon. One million people turned up in Florida to see the start of their journey, but many more welcomed them home. Collins orbited the Moon in the command module while the others explored the lunar surface.

Space travelers

ABOUT 350 HUMANS and countless other living creatures have traveled from Earth into space. All but 26 people, men who went to the Moon, have spent most of their time in space in a craft orbiting Earth. Competition to travel into space is keen. When a call for potential European astronauts was made in the early 1990s, about 20,000 people applied. Six were chosen for training. Astronauts are men and women with an outstanding ability in a scientific discipline, who are both mentally and physically fit. Originally, biologically similar animals were sent into space to test conditions for the first human flight. Now, along with insects and birds, they accompany astronauts and are used for research.

DOG IN SPACE
In Jules Verne book, dog floats in space outside the craft.

Symbol of the International Aeronautical Federation

Passport requests, in five languages, that any necessary help be given to the holder

Photograph of Helen Sharman, British astronaut and owner of this passport

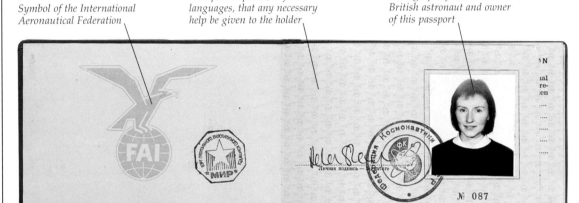

№ 087

PASSPORT TO SPACE
A passport is carried during space travel in case it is needed when the astronaut returns to Earth. An unscheduled landing may be made in a country other than that of the launch. The type shown here is carried by astronauts on Russian craft. The term astronaut describes space travelers from all countries. But those on board Russian craft are also called cosmonauts.

UNTETHERED FLIGHT
Astronauts venturing outside their spacecraft need to be either tethered to the craft or wear a Manned Maneuvering Unit (MMU). It is a powered backpack for traveling free in space. Without it, the astronauts would be "lost" in their own orbit around Earth.

American Bruce McCandless takes first spacewalk that employs a hand-controlled MMU, in 1984

Ham, the first chimpanzee astronaut, or "chimpnaut"

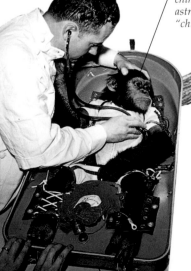

HAM
Chimpanzees were chosen for space travel because their genetic makeup is similar to humans' and because they could be trained to perform tasks. Ham was the first to travel, in January 1961. On his return, he was examined and found to be in excellent condition.

Belka

Strelka

STRELKA AND BELKA
The Soviets launched a number of four-legged astronauts into space. The first living being to travel from Earth was the dog Laika, in 1957 (pp. 18–19). She perished in flight, but two other dogs, Strelka and Belka, returned safely to Earth by parachute in August 1960.

HONEYBEES
In April 1984 a hive of honeybees traveled aboard the space shuttle Challenger. Like most travelers into space, the bees found weightlessness confusing to start with. But once they found their "space wings," they built their honeycomb as successfully as they do on Earth.

Frog is placed in capsule for flight

SPINNING FROGS
Over 20 years ago, two bullfrogs orbited Earth for medical research into the workings of the human inner ear. The frogs were monitored over a five-day period in both weightless and partial-gravity conditions. The frogs were spun in their capsule to create the partial gravity.

Animal and human crews have backups, reserves in case one of the original crew falls sick. This monkey backup is drinking some juice

SQUIRREL MONKEY
The first monkey into space was a squirrel monkey, Gordo, in December 1958. Since then dogs, monkeys, flies, fish, ants, frogs, sea urchins, and over 2,000 jellyfish are only some of the creatures that traveled to space. They have been used for research into various subjects, including the effects of microgravity on fertility and reproduction.

A mask provides oxygen for breathing

Hector, a white rat, was launched from France

READY FOR SPACE
Early animal travelers wore their own spacesuits. Several suits were tested by the Soviets to see which would give their astronaut dogs the most protection. The dogs were chosen because their blood circulation and respiration are similar to our own, and because they are patient creatures.

WHITE RAT
Mice and rats have traveled into space for more than 30 years. One of the first, Hector, a white rat, soared 100 miles (160 km) into space in 1961 and landed safely back on Earth three minutes later, alive and well.

SPACE ZOO
Two monkeys, some snails, beetles, and fruit midges traveled together in December 1996. After a two-week trip to space, they were tested for effects of weightlessness before returning to their Earth zoo. They were loaded on board the Vostok spacecraft in their own capsule. Bone tissue from the monkeys' hip bones, taken before and after the flight, was used for medical research. Monkeys going into space are named in Russian alphabetical order. The winners of a school competition named these two Lapik and Multik.

Man on the Moon

THE MOON IS THE ONLY WORLD that humans have landed on outside our own. For centuries, Earth's companion in space has aroused our interest and, as Earth's nearest neighbor, it was the most likely target for manned space travel. Between 1969 and 1972, twelve American astronauts touched down on the Moon. They traveled there in six separate Apollo missions and spent just over 300 hours on the Moon's surface – 80 hours of that outside the landing craft. They collected rock samples, took photographs, and set up experiments to monitor the Moon's activity and environment. The Apollo missions were followed worldwide.

Apollo 16 lunar module, code-named Orion

Upper part of Orion, which is where astronauts lived while on the Moon, rejoined command module for return journey

Landing legs remained behind when Orion blasted off the Moon and docked with the command module for the return journey

Lunar module is photographed from behind – entrance is on other side

American flag needed small telescopic arm to keep it extended on the airless Moon

Tongs

Communications antenna

Sample bag

Sample return container

Scoops

MOON TOOLS
Rocks and dust were scooped up from the surface or collected in core tubes. Gripping tools against the pressure inside their space gloves gave the astronauts aching forearms and fingernails, which were sore for days.

Hand control

Seating for two astronauts

Room for equipment, tools, bagged rocks and dust samples here and under seat

Television camera

LUNAR ROVER
The astronauts' spacesuits restricted their movement and hindered rock collecting. A light-weight electric car, the Rover, helped the astronauts on Apollo 15, 16, and 17. On the Apollo 16 mission, the Rover covered 16.16 miles (26 km). The top speed achieved was 11 mph (17.7 kmph). The Rover was carried to the Moon folded up in a storage bay of the lunar module.

Large wheels to cope with the Moon's uneven surface

MOON ROCK
Much of the 176 lbs (388 kg) rock collected on the Moon is volcanic. It dates from 3.5 billion years ago.

Neil Armstrong (left) and Buzz Aldrin (right), the first men on the Moon

John Young was the commander of Apollo 16

THE TIMES

Man lands on moon in perfect touchdown

Senator Kennedy to be charged

Suez moves nearer to full-scale war

It looks like a collection of about every kind of rock, Armstrong reports

Who lives in an ivory tower?

HEADLINES AROUND THE WORLD
The world held its breath in July 1969 as Apollo 11 neared the Moon's surface. The successful landing was reported in newspapers and on the radio and television all over the world. Many watched on public screens, others at home. In Tokyo, Japan, shops sold out of color televisions in a pre-launch rush.

APOLLO 16 MOON LANDING
The Apollo craft landed at six different sites. The first three landings were close to the Moon's equator, but later missions carried more fuel and traveled farther. Apollo 16 touched down in the hilly Descartes region, where John Young and Charles Duke explored for three days. Each Apollo landing module had a code name. The first men, Armstrong and Aldrin, landed in Eagle. Apollo 16's lunar module was Orion.

How to be an astronaut

SUSPENDED
As well as learning about spacecraft systems and the theory of working in space, astronauts must practice tasks in space conditions. They can learn what it is like to be in weightless conditions by scuba training or by using equipment like this harness, which helps an astronaut get used to floating free.

MEN AND WOMEN ARE CHOSEN from around the world to train for traveling in space. They are launched aboard either a U.S. space shuttle, where English is the main language, or the Russian Soyuz, where Russian is spoken. The preparations of the two space crews are similar and involve classroom and practical training, including work in mock-ups of the orbiter, Spacelab, and Mir, the Russian space station, and in simulators such as the harness, the 5DF machine, the moon-walker, and the multi-axis wheel, examples of which are found at the Euro Space Center, Transinne, Belgium, and are shown on these two pages. Astronauts can be selected for training every two years. They have a year's basic training, followed by training related to an astronaut's role in space, such as a pilot or mission specialist who performs extravehicular activity (EVA). Only then are the successful astronauts assigned to a flight.

Harness helps astronaut get used to floating free

Three Apollo astronauts in training before their flights to the Moon

JUNGLE EMERGENCY
Astronauts are trained for any kind of situation or emergency. These astronauts are gathering leaves and branches to make a shelter after a simulated emergency landing in the middle of the Panama jungle. Even after landing on Earth, an astronaut's journey may not be over.

LIFE RAFT
Astronaut candidates receive training in parachute jumping and in land and sea survival. American astronaut Leroy Chiao floats in his life raft, in training for an emergency departure from the space shuttle.

MOON-WALKER
Walking in a bulky spacesuit is difficult, particularly on the Moon, where gravity is one-sixth of Earth's. The Apollo astronauts found short hops the best way to get around on the lunar surface. Future trips to the Moon or to Mars can be prepared for by walking in a moon-walker, a suspended chair.

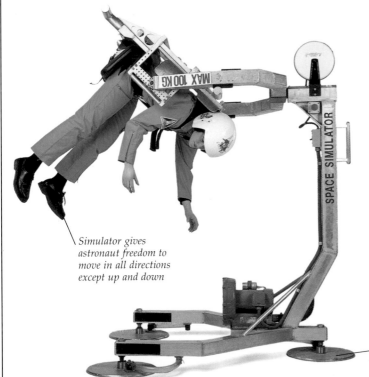

Simulator gives astronaut freedom to move in all directions except up and down

FIVE DEGREES OF FREEDOM
Preparing for the weightlessness of space is not easy. The feeling can be simulated in a chair called the Five Degrees of Freedom (5DF) machine, which allows the astronaut to move in all directions other than up and down without restraint. Alternatively, astronauts can get a 20- to 30-second taste of weightlessness aboard a modified KC-135 jet aircraft as it dives from 35,000 ft (10,668 m) to 24,000 ft (7,315 m). But the experience is brief, even though it can be repeated up to 40 times a day.

Three "feet" float over the floor, simulating movement achieved in frictionless space

UNDERWATER WEIGHTLESSNESS
Spacesuited astronauts can train for EVA in large water tanks, where the sensation of gravity is reduced. Space shuttle astronauts train with full-scale models of the orbiter payload bay and various other payloads. Here engineers work on a space station mock-up in preparation for future missions.

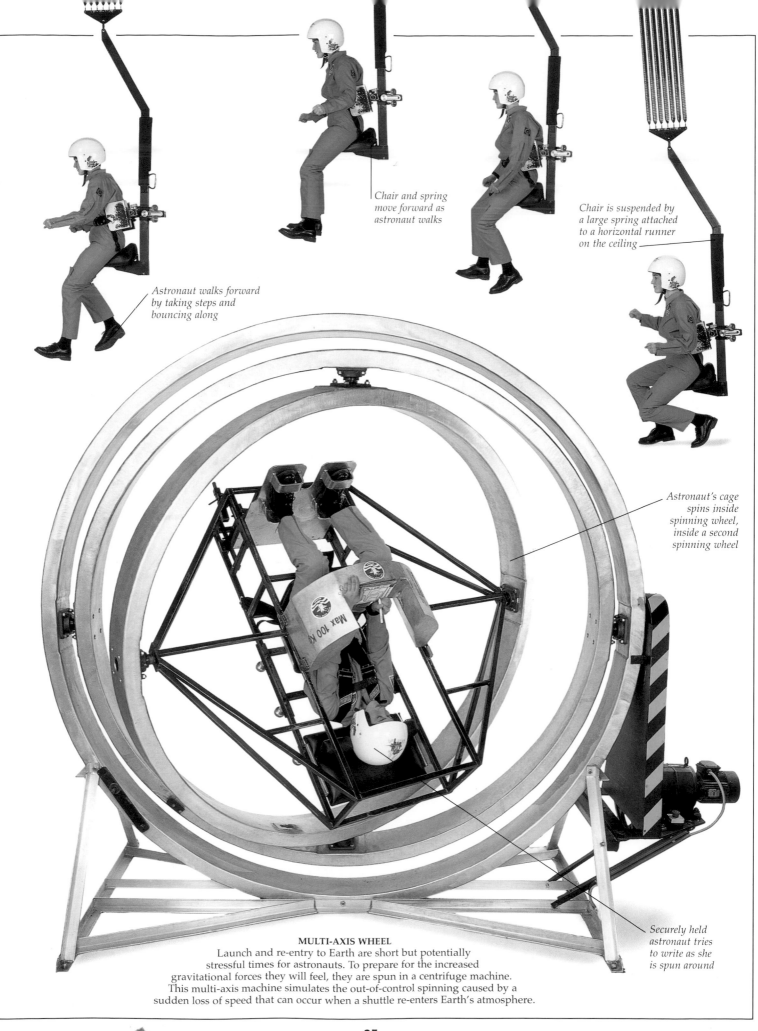

Chair and spring move forward as astronaut walks

Chair is suspended by a large spring attached to a horizontal runner on the ceiling

Astronaut walks forward by taking steps and bouncing along

Astronaut's cage spins inside spinning wheel, inside a second spinning wheel

Max 100 Kg

MULTI-AXIS WHEEL
Launch and re-entry to Earth are short but potentially
stressful times for astronauts. To prepare for the increased
gravitational forces they will feel, they are spun in a centrifuge machine.
This multi-axis machine simulates the out-of-control spinning caused by a
sudden loss of speed that can occur when a shuttle re-enters Earth's atmosphere.

Securely held astronaut tries to write as she is spun around

Astronaut fashion

A SPACESUIT IS LIKE a protective, portable tent that an astronaut wears in space. The first suits were designed for astronauts who were simply flying through space without leaving their craft. The suits they were launched in stayed on during eating, sleeping, going to the toilet, and the return journey. Next came the suit for space itself. This suit provides the astronaut with a personal life support system and protection against temperature extremes and space dust. Before going outside, the suit is pressurized to guard against the near vacuum of space. Today's astronauts wear suits for launch, work outside, and return. Inside, they wear casual, Earthly clothes.

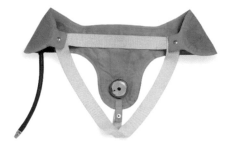

Urine transferred from here

MOBILE MAN
The first spacesuits were based on high-altitude jet aircraft pressure suits. Astronauts wearing them had to be able to bend their arms and legs. The Apollo suits for the Moon had bellows-like molded rubber joints. The design has been simplified in this toy from 1966.

Male underpants, designed for thermal control, 1960

Device for collecting urine for male astronauts, early 1960s

SPACE UNDERWEAR
Coping with human waste presents a tricky design problem. Any collecting device needs to keep the astronaut comfortable and dry. Collecting devices were essential for astronauts on early craft without toilets and, today, for long periods spent outside the craft.

Portable life support system

Suit of Yuri Gagarin, first man in space, in 1961

Aleksei Leonov's suit, the first to be used outside a spacecraft, in 1965

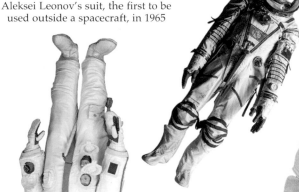

Oleg Makarov's suit, used between 1973 and 1980

All-in-one overshoe has sole and heel

Mir space station suit, used in the late 1980s

CHANGING FASHION
A spacesuit's main job is to protect an astronaut. But it must also allow its wearer to move about easily. These two basic requirements have not changed since the first astronaut flew. Yet, as the suits here show, spacesuit design has changed. New materials and techniques and practical experience combine to produce a comfortable and efficient suit for today's working astronaut. A suit is no longer tailor-made for one person but off-the-rack, and can be reused by another astronaut.

Overshoe kept in place by snap fasteners on back of ankle

Oxygen passed to helmet through channels in internal surface

Visor's gold coating reflects heat and light

LOUSMA

DESIGNED FOR THE MOON
The Apollo suits were designed for use on the Moon. Closest to the skin, the astronaut wore a one-piece lightweight garment with sensors for monitoring changes in his body. Next was a garment with a network of 300 ft (91.44 m) of tubing with constantly circulating cool water to maintain the astronaut's correct body temperature. On top came the suit, made of strong synthetic fibers, metals, and plastics. A portable life support system was added on the back and controlled from the chest of the suit when the astronauts went outside their craft.

Outer helmet

Pressure helmet

Communications cap

Pen-light pocket

Two-piece underwear – a long-sleeved vest and full-length pants

One-piece suit and underwear worn under spacesuit for launch and return home

Flag of Great Britain

Х. ШАРМАН
H. SHARMAN

Unisex one-piece has underleg zip for quicker waste removal

Outer glove placed over an inner pressure glove

IN-FLIGHT SPACE CLOTHES
Astronauts now have a variety of clothes they can wear inside a spacecraft. In the warm, safe atmosphere of a shuttle orbiter or a space station, astronauts wear unisex T-shirts and shorts or jogging pants. Socks keep feet warm, but there is no need for shoes. Helen Sharman's in-flight clothes included this one-piece sleeveless suit and jacket. In fact, it was far too warm on Mir to wear them together when she stayed on the station in 1991.

GEMINI SUIT
A member of the team who designed and made the suits for American astronauts in the 1960s tests a Gemini suit. It was worn by the first Americans to walk in space outside their craft.

Outer layers offer protection against temperature extremes and space dust

Foot strap holds trouser in place

Pocket contents secured by zip fastener

Living in space

ALL THE THINGS THAT WE DO on Earth to stay alive are also done by astronauts in space. Astronauts still need to eat, breathe, sleep, keep clean and healthy, and use the toilet. Everything needed for these activities is transported to, or made in, space. The main difference between life on Earth and life in space is weightlessness. Seemingly simple, everyday tasks, such as breathing, need to be carefully thought out. As the astronauts use up oxygen and breathe out carbon dioxide, they are in danger of suffocating. Fresh oxygen is circulated through the craft. Water vapor from the astronauts' breath is collected and recycled for use in experiments and for drinking. Air rather than water is used to suck, instead of flush, body wastes away.

WITHOUT SETTLING
In a spacecraft, anything not tied down will move around with the slightest push. Dust does not settle and so must be vacuumed out of the air.

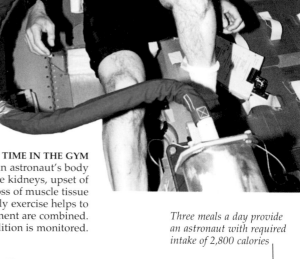

UNDER PRESSURE
Body fluids, no longer pulled down by gravity, flow toward an astronaut's head. For the first few days the face looks fatter and the nasal passages are blocked. Belts worn at the top of each leg help control the flow of fluids until the body adjusts itself.

TIME IN THE GYM
The upward movement of fluids in an astronaut's body causes excretion of more urine by the kidneys, upset of the body's salt concentration, and loss of muscle tissue and function. About two hours of daily exercise helps to counteract this. Here exercise and experiment are combined. As Canadian Robert Thirsk pedals, his condition is monitored.

Three meals a day provide an astronaut with required intake of 2,800 calories

Pineapple

Peach

Sweet-and-sour beef

Drinks

Pear

Rice

Fruit and nuts

Chicken

Cereals

WHAT'S ON THE MENU?
Meals are prepared long before launch. Packaged foods may be ready to eat, or need warming, or need water added. Many foods, such as cornflakes, meatballs, and lemon pudding, are similar to those on a supermarket shelf. Fresh foods are eaten at the start of a trip or when delivered by visiting astronauts.

Food packages held on tray, which is strapped to astronaut's leg

Peas

Almonds

Holes in the cutlery handles allow them to be tied down

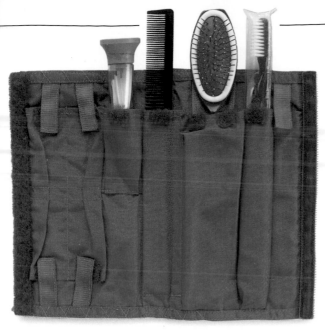

PERSONAL HYGIENE
Astronauts' clothes are unisex, but personal hygiene items are not – male astronauts can carry razors. Astronauts flying to Mir are given a cloth pouch with hair-, tooth-, and hand-care items. Teeth are cleaned with a brush and edible, non-frothy toothpaste, or with a saturated washcloth.

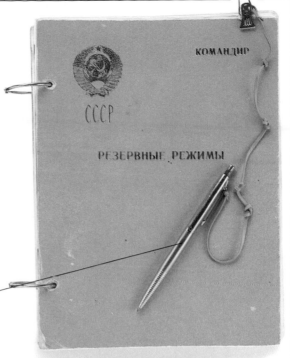

In pens designed for space, ink is pushed toward nib. On Earth, gravity pulls ink down

ASTRONAUT'S LOG
An astronaut's logbook contains details of flight procedures. Helen Sharman followed the launch, Mir docking, and Earth landing in hers. She flew to Mir on the Russian craft Soyuz TM-12. As part of her training, she had learned to speak Russian.

HIGH-FLYING BUTTERFLY
Everything an astronaut might need in space is provided by the space agency he or she is flying with. But astronauts do have a chance to take a personal item or two with them. These must be small and light. Helen Sharman carried this brooch given to her by her father.

Body-washing wipe

SPACE SHOWER
The first private toilet and shower were on the American space station Skylab, which was in use in 1973-74. The toilet was unreliable and disturbed other astronauts when in use. The shower proved leaky, and astronauts spent precious time cleaning up. The Americans decided to do without one in the shuttle system, and the one on Mir is rarely used.

KEEPING CLEAN
Wet wipes are used to clean astronauts' bodies and the inside of the spacecraft. Some, like these Russian ones, are specially made for use in space. Others are commercial baby wipes.

American astronaut Jack Lousma uses shower on Skylab

Inside sealed unit, water is air-blasted at astronaut and immediately sucked up

Handle for astronaut to hold him- or herself down

Astronaut sits here; toilet seat is lifted up for cleaning

Toilet is cut away to show how the solid waste is collected

Male or female funnel is held close to the astronaut to collect liquid waste

WASTE MANAGEMENT
To use the toilet, an astronaut puts on a rubber glove and chooses a funnel. Once this is fitted to the waste hose, he or she sits down and holds the funnel close to his or her body. The toilet fan is turned on, and when the astronaut urinates, the liquid is drawn through the hose by air. Before discarding solid waste, the toilet bowl is pressurized to produce a tight seal between the astronaut and the seat. Finally, the astronaut cleans his or her self and the toilet with wipes.

Hose takes away liquid waste

Feet are secured on the footrests

Model of space toilet from Euro Space Center, Transinne, Belgium

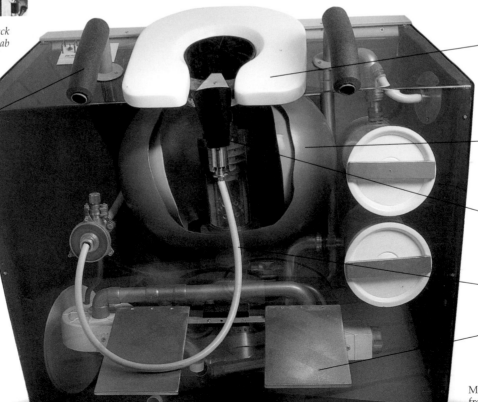

Astronauts at work

A WORKING DAY FOR ASTRONAUTS could be spent inside or outside the spacecraft. Inside, routine monitoring and maintenance on the craft are carried out alongside scientific testing and experimentation. Activities such as investigating the effects of space travel on the human body, testing new products for use in space, and doing research in food production will benefit future space generations. Commercial organizations send experiments into space to be performed in weightlessness. Work outside a craft is called Extravehicular Activity (EVA). Out in space astronauts are either tethered to their craft or wear a Manned Maneuvering Unit (MMU), a powered backpack. They might be deploying satellites, setting up experiments, or building new space stations.

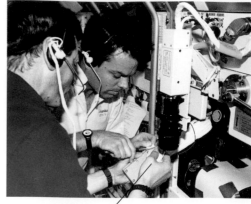

Repair of the Bubble Drop Particle Unit

RUNNING REPAIRS
In-flight repairs had to be made to an experiment unit on board Columbia. Back on Earth, Spanish astronaut Pedro Duque carried out the repair procedure on a duplicate unit. His work was recorded, and the video pictures were transmitted to the in-flight crew, Frenchman Jean-Jacques Favier and American Kevin Kregel, who then did the real repair.

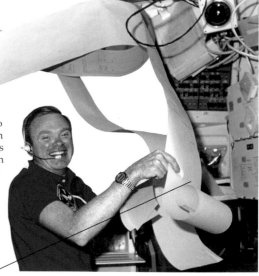

ORDERS FROM BELOW
Astronauts are assigned tasks on a mission long before they leave Earth. This can mean working closely with the scientists and engineers who have designed and produced experiments in the months prior to launch. Once the astronauts are in space, the scientists wait anxiously on Earth for the successful completion of the mission. In the meantime, they can stay in touch through the teleprinter.

Goggles and headgear examine how the astronaut orients

American astronaut Richard Linnehan in Spacelab aboard Columbia

Challenger was filled with hundreds of yards' worth of paper in 1985

LOOK AFTER YOURSELF
For some work, the astronauts are both the scientists and the subjects of their investigations. Their job is to see how human bodies – their own – cope with the space environment. On Earth, gravity pulls things toward its surface and so provides a visual reference for up and down. In space, there is no up and down.

Astronaut prepares samples in the glove box

WORKING IN A GLOVE BOX
Experiments from around the world are carried out in Mir, or aboard an American space shuttle. They usually take place in Spacelab (right), the European laboratory. Some tests only need to be activated when in space; others need more direct participation by an astronaut. American astronaut Leroy Chiao (top) places samples in one of the centrifuges on board. American Donald Thomas's hands are in the glove box, a sealed experiment unit (pp. 38–39).

Securing pins

Sheet cutters

Bolt tightener

Wire cutters

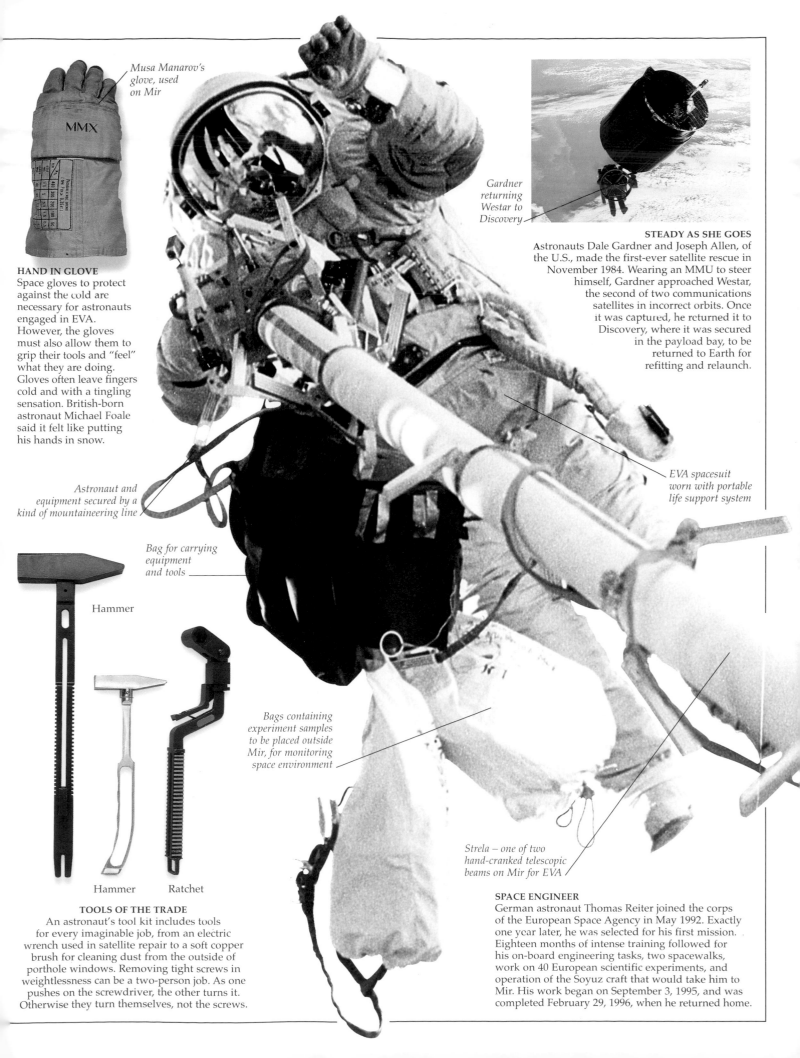

HAND IN GLOVE
Space gloves to protect against the cold are necessary for astronauts engaged in EVA. However, the gloves must also allow them to grip their tools and "feel" what they are doing. Gloves often leave fingers cold and with a tingling sensation. British-born astronaut Michael Foale said it felt like putting his hands in snow.

Musa Manarov's glove, used on Mir

Gardner returning Westar to Discovery

STEADY AS SHE GOES
Astronauts Dale Gardner and Joseph Allen, of the U.S., made the first-ever satellite rescue in November 1984. Wearing an MMU to steer himself, Gardner approached Westar, the second of two communications satellites in incorrect orbits. Once it was captured, he returned it to Discovery, where it was secured in the payload bay, to be returned to Earth for refitting and relaunch.

EVA spacesuit worn with portable life support system

Astronaut and equipment secured by a kind of mountaineering line

Bag for carrying equipment and tools

Hammer

Hammer   Ratchet

TOOLS OF THE TRADE
An astronaut's tool kit includes tools for every imaginable job, from an electric wrench used in satellite repair to a soft copper brush for cleaning dust from the outside of porthole windows. Removing tight screws in weightlessness can be a two-person job. As one pushes on the screwdriver, the other turns it. Otherwise they turn themselves, not the screws.

Bags containing experiment samples to be placed outside Mir, for monitoring space environment

Strela – one of two hand-cranked telescopic beams on Mir for EVA

SPACE ENGINEER
German astronaut Thomas Reiter joined the corps of the European Space Agency in May 1992. Exactly one year later, he was selected for his first mission. Eighteen months of intense training followed for his on-board engineering tasks, two spacewalks, work on 40 European scientific experiments, and operation of the Soyuz craft that would take him to Mir. His work began on September 3, 1995, and was completed February 29, 1996, when he returned home.

Rest and play

Yo-yo thrown out sideways comes back without gravity pulling it down

ASTRONAUTS HAVE LEISURE TIME in space just as they would if they were down on Earth. When the day's work is finished, they might indulge in a favorite pastime, such as reading, photography, or music – or join together for a game of cards. Whatever their preference, they are bound to spend some time simply gazing out of the spacecraft window. Watching the world far below is a pastime no astronaut tires of. When the first astronauts went into space, they had every moment of their time accounted for and ground control was always listening in. Time to unwind and enjoy the experience and unique sensations space offers is now in every astronaut's timetable.

SEEING SHARKS
American astronaut Bill Lenoir watches his rubber shark.

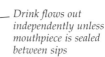

WRITING HOME
Laptop computers help astronauts stay in touch with family and friends on a day-to-day basis. Others prefer to write letters home. Astronauts on Mir operate their own post office. Letters are stamped and dated when written and handed over when the astronaut gets back to Earth. This French stamp celebrates communication.

REPUBLIQUE FRANÇAISE / MEZIERES / POSTES 1988 / LA COMMUNICATION 2,20

Jacks float in midair, since there is no gravity to keep them on a surface

A chain of seven magnetic marbles is achieved on Earth before gravity pulls them apart

In space, because the marbles are weightless, you can keep on adding to the chain

STAY STILL!
On Earth, jacks are picked up in increasing numbers from the floor as the ball is thrown up and caught. In space, the jacks are released in midair but always drift apart. The ball is thrown to a spacecraft wall and caught on its return journey.

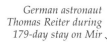

Drink flows out independently unless mouthpiece is sealed between sips

Coke Coca-Cola — Trade-mark® — 12 FL OZ 354 mL

SNACKTIME
Hungry astronauts have a choice of snacks and drinks to have between meals. Dried fruit, nuts, crumb-free cookie bars, and hot or cold drinks supplement their diet. Drinks are usually taken from sealed packs or tubes. Once this soda can is opened in space, the drink can flow out freely, so it needs a special mouthpiece.

Guitar collapses for easy storage

German astronaut Thomas Reiter during 179-day stay on Mir

COSMIC CHORDS
Music tapes are light and small, two important qualities for any non-essential item carried into space. Singing along can be fun, but as one astronaut relaxes, another is still working hard only feet away, so the volume cannot be too high. Sometimes a change of tune is supplied by visiting astronauts. In November 1995, an Atlantis crew briefly docked with Mir, leaving behind a gift of a collapsible guitar.

SPACE TOYS
Ten familiar toys were packed aboard the space shuttle Discovery when it blasted into space in April 1985. These ten, plus one more the astronauts made in space, a paper airplane, became the stars of an educational video. The mid-deck became a classroom as the astronauts demonstrated the toys, including a yo-yo, jacks, and magnetic marbles.

Hair only moves upward if pushed

HAIR-RAISING
Washing clothes and hair are not top priorities in space. Clothes are bagged and brought home dirty. Hair washing can be avoided if the trip is short. If it needs to be washed, it cannot be done in the usual way, with lots of water and shampoo. Dirt can be wiped away by a cloth impregnated with a shampoo-like substance.

Susan Helms, American, tests space shampoo

Inflatable ring provides support for the sleeping astronaut

Wubbo Ockels from the Netherlands on board space shuttle Challenger in 1985

Woolly slippers gave Ockels extra warmth and comfort

SPACE PHOTOGRAPHER
Taking photographs in space is one way to keep a unique memory alive. Cameras for prints, slides, videos, and movies are on board the spacecraft. As well as making an official record of the trip, astronauts take fun shots. American Karl Henize photographs through the window of the Challenger shuttle orbiter to catch the scene in the payload bay outside.

Sleeping bag designed by Wubbo Ockels

GOODNIGHT, SLEEP TIGHT
Astronauts once slept in their seats or in temporarily hung hammocks. Today they have a more comfortable choice. Sleeping bags are attached to the walls of the spacecraft, or a sound-suppression blanket and sheets with weightlessness restraints are used in a private bunk bed. This special sleeping bag was used in the 1980s aboard the space shuttle and Mir. Its inflatable ring simulates the pressure that the weight of bedclothes provides on Earth.

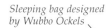

Danger and disaster

GREAT CARE IS TAKEN IN THE PLANNING and preparation of a space mission. Once a rocket and its cargo leave the ground, there is little anyone can do if things go terribly wrong. The smallest error can mean the end of a billion-dollar project. Years of work and the hopes and expectations of countless people can be lost in a second. Mistakes happen and problems do arise, ranging from an astronaut's cold delaying a flight, through whole projects failing, to the loss of life. But big disasters are rare, and we are incredibly successful at sending craft and astronauts into space.

NEIGHBORS
The American shuttle launch center is in Florida, next to a wildlife refuge. The osprey is one of over 300 species of birds in the area. Space technicians check regularly to see that the birds do not nest in the wrong place.

PARACHUTE PROBLEM
Vladimir Komarov was the first human to be killed in space flight. After a day in space, he descended to Earth on April 24, 1967. The lines of his Soyuz 1 parachute became tangled and the parachute deflated. The craft plunged to the ground and burst into flames.

The Apollo 13 crew are honored. Their mission was regarded as a successful failure because of the rescue experience gained

President Nixon welcomes home the crew of Apollo 13

MISSION ABORT
On April 13, 1970, two days after launch, Apollo 13's journey to the Moon was interrupted when an oxygen tank ruptured and caused an explosion. It damaged power and life-support systems on board. This severe emergency was calmly reported to Earth with the words "Houston, we have a problem." The planned lunar landing was abandoned and every effort was channeled into getting the three-man crew home safely.

John Swigert   Fred Haise   James Lovell   Richard Nixon

HOME AT LAST
The explosion aboard Apollo 13 was in the service module and put its engine out of action. The astronauts used the engine of the lunar module, originally intended for maneuver on and off the Moon, to take them around the Moon and return them to Earth. Everyone was relieved as the astronauts were lifted aboard the recovery ship.

FLASH FIRE
Astronauts Virgil Grissom, Edward White, and Roger Chaffee perished in a fire in the command module of the American Apollo 1 on January 27, 1967. They were on the ground, practicing launch countdown. The astronauts could not open the module hatch to escape. Spacecraft were redesigned.

Effects of the intense heat can be seen on the outside of the command module

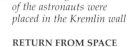

Urns holding the remains of the astronauts were placed in the Kremlin wall

RETURN FROM SPACE
After a 23-day stay aboard the Salyut 1 space station, Soviet astronauts Georgi Dobrovolsky, Vladislav Volkov, and Viktor Patsayev started their journey home. As they approached Earth on June 30, 1971, air escaped from their capsule. The three were not wearing spacesuits, suffocated, and were found dead when their capsule landed.

Astronauts test launch pad emergency exit in a dress rehearsal for their launch

One of seven baskets. Each basket can hold three crew members and has its own wire system to carry it safely to the ground

Personalized badge was made to commemorate a teacher – rather than a regularly trained astronaut – going into space

Challenger, the space shuttle orbiter, first flew in 1983. This 1986 flight was its tenth mission into space

The NASA – National Aeronautics and Space Administration – logo

ESCAPE ROUTE

Emergency procedures have been developed to allow astronauts to get away from their craft quickly. For shuttle astronauts, the escape route before the final 30 seconds of countdown, practiced here, is via a steel-wire basket. It takes 35 seconds to slide to the ground. On arrival, the astronauts move to an emergency bunker until they get the all-clear.

LOST IN SPACE

In February 1996, astronauts were putting a satellite into space when the 12.8-mile (20.6-km) tether that connected it to the space shuttle Columbia snapped. The $442 million satellite had to be given up as lost. Astronauts had unsuccessfully tried to deploy the Italian satellite four years earlier. If deployed, the satellite would have been swept through Earth's magnetic field to generate electricity.

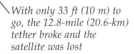

With only 33 ft (10 m) to go, the 12.8-mile (20.6-km) tether broke and the satellite was lost

CHALLENGER TRAGEDY

Seventy-three seconds after liftoff on January 28, 1986, the space shuttle Challenger exploded. All seven of the crew were killed, including teacher Sharon Christa McAuliffe. She had won a national contest to be the first civilian to travel aboard the shuttle and was planning to teach a class from space. Launch pad preparation and liftoff are among the most dangerous parts of a mission. This was the first flight to take off and not reach space.

Mars-96 was assembled at the Lavochkin Scientific-Industrial Association, Khimki, near Moscow

MARS-96

The Russian space probe Mars-96 was launched successfully from the Baikonur space center on November 16, 1996, but about half an hour after takeoff, contact with the probe was lost. The fourth set of boosters had failed to lift Mars-96 out of Earth orbit and on toward Mars.

PECKING PROBLEM

A yellow-shafted flicker delayed the launch of the space shuttle Discovery in June 1995. It was ready for liftoff on the launch pad but had to be returned to its hangar at a cost of $100,000. The bird, a woodpecker, had pecked more than 75 holes in the fuel tank's insulating foam. Plastic owls are among the measures now taken to avoid repetition of the problem.

Experiment box recovered from swamps in French Guiana, near launch site of Ariane 5

LOST PROPERTY

The failure of Mars-96 was a serious setback for the exploration of Mars and the Russian space program. The probe had been scheduled to land four probes on Mars in September 1997. The loss of experiments on this probe came only five months after the destruction of experiments carried on the European Space Agency (ESA)'s Ariane 5, which blew up soon after launch as a result of a computer software problem.

Space stations

Аʙоuт 250 miles (400 km) above Earth, a space station orbits the planet every 92 minutes. Its name is Mir, and it has been there since February 1986. A space station such as Mir is a space home. Astronauts can be on board for months at a time. They carry out experiments, make observations, and collect valuable data on how humans cope with long-term space life. The records for the most hours in space and the longest unbroken stay by one person were made on Mir. It is Russia's eighth space station; the earlier ones were all named Salyut. The U.S. had one station in the 1970s, Skylab. Today its astronauts spend time and do their work on Mir.

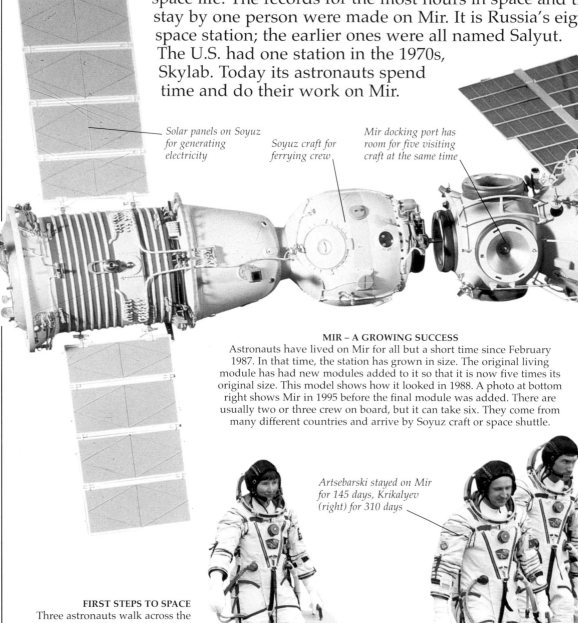

First Mir module into space; crew live here

Solar panels on Soyuz for generating electricity

Soyuz craft for ferrying crew

Mir docking port has room for five visiting craft at the same time

MIR – A GROWING SUCCESS
Astronauts have lived on Mir for all but a short time since February 1987. In that time, the station has grown in size. The original living module has had new modules added to it so that it is now five times its original size. This model shows how it looked in 1988. A photo at bottom right shows Mir in 1995 before the final module was added. There are usually two or three crew on board, but it can take six. They come from many different countries and arrive by Soyuz craft or space shuttle.

Artsebarski stayed on Mir for 145 days, Krikalyev (right) for 310 days

FIRST STEPS TO SPACE
Three astronauts walk across the Baikonur launch site toward their Soyuz TM-12 rocket to take them to Mir in May 1991. Helen Sharman (left) from Great Britain was the first woman on Mir; she stayed on board for eight days. The commander, Anatoli Artsebarski, like Sharman, was flying for the first time. Flight engineer Sergei Krikalyev (right) was familiar with Mir, as he had stayed there two years earlier.

Spacesuits are fireproof, waterproof, airtight, and ventilated. The helmet goes on last

THE HIGH LIFE

The seventh and final Salyut space station was launched in April 1982. Salyut 7 was in orbit about 200 miles (320 km) above Earth until February 1991. The first crew were Anatoly Berezovoi (top) and Valentin Lebedev. They spent 211 days in space, setting a record. It was also home to the first male female crew in space.

POSTCARD FROM SPACE

Cards like this one have been through a post office that is truly out of this world – the one on board Mir. The office's unique postmark is stamped by hand. The crew aboard Mir in late 1987 stamped and signed about 1,000 envelopes for stamp collectors around the world.

Sergei Avdeev stayed on Mir from September 1995 to February 1996

Signed by each astronaut on board Mir

INSIDE MIR

The inside of Mir is similar in shape and size to the inside of a railroad car. There is no floor or ceiling, so in every direction there is equipment for the operation of the space station, for experiments, or for the astronauts' day-to-day needs.

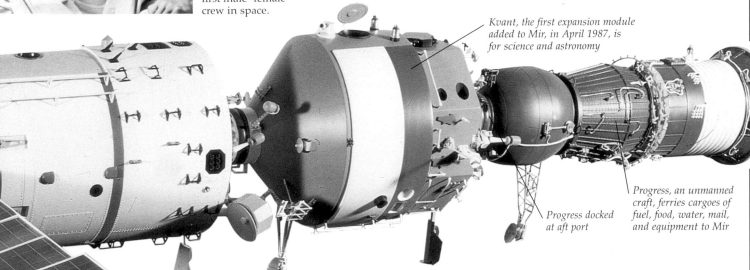

Kvant, the first expansion module added to Mir, in April 1987, is for science and astronomy

Progress docked at aft port

Progress, an unmanned craft, ferries cargoes of fuel, food, water, mail, and equipment to Mir

SPACE UNION

In June 1995, an American space shuttle docked with Mir for the first time. Together they made the largest spacecraft ever in orbit. The crew aboard the American craft, Atlantis, had their own celebration – they were the 100th American human space launch.

Photograph of Atlantis moving away from Mir, taken by Solovyev and Budarin, who temporarily left Mir in their Soyuz spacecraft

HITCHING A RIDE

Anatoly Solovyev and Nikolai Budarin were taken to Mir aboard Atlantis. Once the orbiter had docked with Mir, the hatches on each side were opened. Solovyev and Budarin and the five American crew members passed through to Mir for a welcoming ceremony. Five days later, Atlantis, carrying the Americans, left Mir, leaving the other two behind.

FOND FAREWELL

Atlantis and Mir were docked together for about 100 hours as they orbited Earth in June 1995. On board were the seven astronauts who had arrived on Atlantis, and three other astronauts who were already in Mir. These three prepared for re-entry into gravity after more than three months in space. They returned to Earth aboard Atlantis with the medical samples they had taken while in space.

Science without gravity

Badge for
Spacelab 2 of 1985

ASTRONAUTS MONITOR, control, and perform experiments inside and outside their craft as they orbit Earth. The experiments are provided by space agencies, industry, universities, and schools. They may be concerned with finding out how living things, like astronauts, insects, and plants, cope in space, or may cover subjects such as chemical processes and the behavior of materials. The knowledge acquired is used for planning the future of space travel or is applied to life on Earth. Experiments may be only a part of a crew's workload or the whole reason for a space mission.

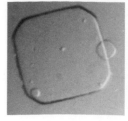

CRYSTAL
This is a space-grown human-body plasma protein crystal. Crystals grown in space are larger and better ordered than those grown on Earth. Studying them provides knowledge needed to produce medicines for the human body.

Bondar checks on oat seedlings in an experiment box aboard Discovery

SPACELAB
A laboratory designed for space, Spacelab flies in the payload bay of the space shuttle. It is a pressurized cabin where astronauts work. In addition, U-shaped pallets outside the cabin hold instruments for direct exposure to space. It first flew in 1983. An average flight lasts ten days. Here the ESA laboratory is being fitted into the shuttle's payload bay before a flight.

GROWING FOOD
A self-contained plant-growth unit was used in March 1982 to test how weightlessness affects plants. These two sets of seedlings were grown from seeds in the unit aboard Columbia. They grew to look much the same as seedlings growing on Earth, although a few small roots grew upward.

EXPERIMENT IN A BOX
Canadian Roberta Bondar was one of seven astronauts performing experiments during an eight-day shuttle flight in January 1992. Their research included the effects of weightlessness on lentil and oat seedlings and on shrimp and fruit fly eggs.

Oat seedlings

Mung bean seedlings

BABY BOOM
The first Earth creature to be born in space emerged from its shell on March 22, 1990. The quail chick was the result of an experiment aboard Mir. Forty-eight Japanese quail eggs had been flown to the space station and placed inside a special incubator with ventilation, feeding, heating, waste removal, and storage systems attached. Then astronauts on Mir and scientists on Earth waited. On the 17th day, the first eggs began to crack open and six chicks broke free, one after the other. The birth made little impact beyond the world of space biologists, but it marked a key moment in research into reproduction in space, which will be used to plan for the future.

Quail's egg with crack
as it begins to hatch

Chick's feathers
appear as egg breaks

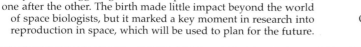

WORKING TOGETHER – THE EXPERIMENT

An astronaut performs experiments in space on behalf of an Earth-based scientist. Above, a scientist (right) instructs the astronaut who is going to be in charge of his telescope in space. They are checking the controls for pointing the telescope at the correct part of the Sun.

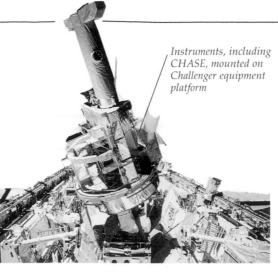

Instruments, including CHASE, mounted on Challenger equipment platform

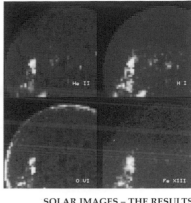

CHASE – THE INSTRUMENT

The second Spacelab mission, which flew aboard *Challenger* in summer 1985, included the scientist's telescope in the orbiter payload bay. The telescope, called the Coronal Helium Abundance Spacelab Experiment (CHASE), measured the amount of helium in the Sun's outer layers.

SOLAR IMAGES – THE RESULTS

CHASE made these images of the Sun. They are in false color to bring out details. The images are of the Sun's outer gas layer, the corona. Each image depicts a different height within the corona. The images are of a particularly active part of the corona and reveal the structure of the Sun's magnetic field.

ALL IN A DAY'S WORK

The French astronaut Jean-Jacques Favier works on an experiment while wearing the Torso Rotation Experiment, which is one of a series of devices used to study the effects of weightlessness on the human body. Favier and other crew members in the Life and Microgravity Spacelab aboard *Columbia* in 1996 were also tested for bone tissue loss, muscle performance, and energy expenditure.

Richard Linnehan, an American, tests his muscle response with the handgrip equipment

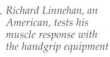

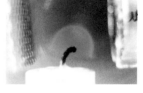

CANDLE FLAMES

It is known that factors such as gravity and airflow influence the spread of an Earth fire, but what might affect a space fire? Tests have shown that space flames form a sphere rather than the pointed shape they have on Earth (left). They also lean strongly when subjected to an electric field (right), which has no effect on Earth flames.

Astronauts use foot grips to keep themselves steady as they work

Torso Rotation Experiment

Arabella in the web she built on board Skylab

ARABELLA THE SPIDER

One space science experiment was designed by a high-school student in Massachusetts. It involved two spiders, Anita and Arabella. The student wanted to find out how well they could make webs in weightless conditions. Their first attempts at web spinning were not perfect, but once the spiders adapted to space, they built strong and well-organized webs.

Chick squeezes out of broken egg

Eggshell falls away as chick is hatched

Quail chick stands up

Testing equipment

ANY EQUIPMENT SENT into space undergoes rigorous and lengthy tests long before it gets near the launch site. The process of building and testing for space starts years ahead of liftoff. Prototypes of each element of a space probe or satellite are individually built and thoroughly tested before moving on to produce the actual flight parts. About a year before launch, the parts are brought together for assembly. The whole craft is then put through another test cycle to ensure that it is fully spaceworthy. It must be able to withstand both the stress of launch and the environment once in space. The tests are therefore carried out in conditions as close as possible to those encountered in space.

TESTING SPACECRAFT
At its Netherlands space center, the European Space Agency (ESA) monitors and analyzes the behavior of space probes and satellites to assess how spaceworthy the craft are. Something as simple as a speck of dust can cause a very costly short circuit later on, so the tests are carried out in clean conditions.

Exterior of the LSS, shown in detail below

Facilities for testing small- and medium-sized equipment

HUMAN TESTS
In 1968, American John Bull tested a newly designed Apollo spacesuit for mobility. Bull later withdrew from training because of poor health and never made it into space. Men and women traveling into space also go through test procedures to make sure they are in good condition and will survive their trip.

ADAPTING TO SPACE
With more, and longer, space flights planned, astronauts are increasingly being tested for endurance and adaptability. They undergo tests before, during, and after flight. Tests are carried out on other humans for comparison. Volunteers are strapped down, wired up, and swung about to simulate the return from space to gravity.

LARGE SPACE SIMULATOR
The environmental conditions a craft will encounter in space are simulated by special test equipment. The European Space Agency has been using the Large Space Simulator (LSS) since 1986 to test its space probes and satellites. It works by re-creating the vacuum, heat, and solar radiation conditions of space. The craft to be tested is sealed in the main chamber, which is depressurized to achieve a vacuum. The impact of the Sun is produced by lamps, with a large mirror directing the solar beam to the craft. This is a model of the LSS that allows you to see inside.

Chambers have temperature-controlled stainless steel shrouds

Light reflection from sun simulator is directed to main chamber

Auxiliary chamber houses mirror

Mirror is made up of 121 pieces

Test using thin metal   Test using thick metal

GAS GUN
Spacecraft need to be protected from minuscule particles of space dust, which can produce surface holes and craters when they collide with the craft. Scientists in Canterbury, England, use a gas gun to assess the damage such particles can cause. This research has provided valuable information for the design of spacecraft bumper shields.

BUMPER SHIELD
• Scientists have tested different thicknesses of metal to find a way of minimizing the damage dust particles can do to space probes. A double-layer bumper shield can also reduce damage. The first layer of metal breaks up the particle and spreads out the energy of impact.

SOLAR PANELS
The contrast of these two solar panels shows the effects of space. The piece on the right has not been used, whereas the piece on the left has been retrieved from space. The dents and pits caused by the impact of space particles can be clearly seen. Scientists can use this evidence to determine the size and speed of the particles.

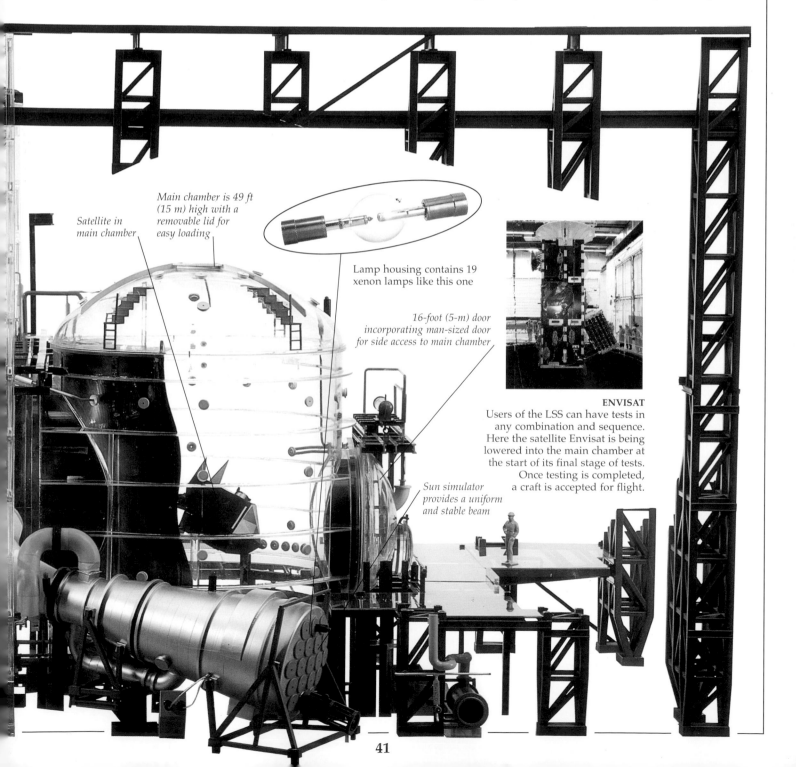

Satellite in main chamber

Main chamber is 49 ft (15 m) high with a removable lid for easy loading

Lamp housing contains 19 xenon lamps like this one

16-foot (5-m) door incorporating man-sized door for side access to main chamber

Sun simulator provides a uniform and stable beam

ENVISAT
Users of the LSS can have tests in any combination and sequence. Here the satellite Envisat is being lowered into the main chamber at the start of its final stage of tests. Once testing is completed, a craft is accepted for flight.

Lone explorers

VOYAGER 1
Two Voyager craft toured Jupiter, Saturn, Uranus, and Neptune.

Rᴏʙᴏᴛɪᴄ ꜱᴘᴀᴄᴇᴄʀᴀꜰᴛ ᴇxᴘʟᴏʀᴇ ꜱᴘᴀᴄᴇ for us. About the size of family cars, they are launched from Earth by rocket or space shuttle to travel to a predetermined target. On board these space probes is scientific equipment to carry out investigations, a power supply, small thruster rockets for path adjustment, and means for recording and sending data back to Earth. A probe may fly by its target or orbit it. Some carry a second, smaller probe or lander craft for release into an atmosphere or for a touchdown on a planetary or lunar surface. Probes have investigated all Solar System planets except Pluto, have taken a close look at two comets, two asteroids, many moons, and the Sun.

SOAKING UP THE SUN
The Solar and Heliospheric Observatory (SOHO), the most comprehensive spacecraft to study the Sun, started its work in April 1996. Twelve different instruments on board the SOHO space probe are observing the Sun constantly.

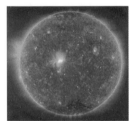

SUNNY OUTLOOK
In visible light the Sun appears calm, but SOHO is recording plenty of vigorous activity. Every day, SOHO pictures the whole Sun at four ultraviolet wavelengths (shown here), which correspond to different temperatures in the Sun's atmosphere. When SOHO started work, the Sun was in the quietest phase of its 11-year cycle, so plenty of action was still to come.

Circles represent hydrogen atoms emitting radiation at its characteristic wavelength

Sketch of Pioneer, drawn to scale, with people to show size of a human

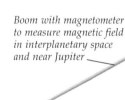

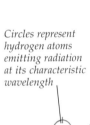

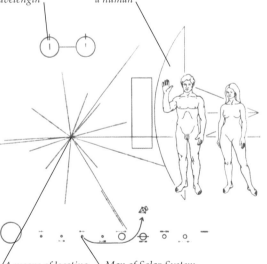

A means of locating the Solar System in the Milky Way

Map of Solar System showing Pioneer has come from third planet (Earth) and passed close by Jupiter

MESSAGE FROM EARTH
A few months before the launch of Pioneer 10 in 1972, it was realized that it and its sister probe, Pioneer 11, would follow paths that would eventually take them out of the Solar System. It was agreed that the probes, traveling in opposite directions, should carry messages in case any extraterrestrials come across them in the future. The messages were etched on a 6 in (15 cm) x 9 in (23 cm) gold-covered aluminum plaque.

Boom with magnetometer to measure magnetic field in interplanetary space and near Jupiter

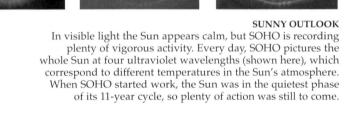

BEYOND THE BELT
Pioneer 10 left Earth on March 3, 1972, for a journey to Jupiter. It was the first probe to venture beyond the asteroid belt. It took six months to emerge on the far side, successfully avoiding a collision with a piece of space rock. The probe flew by Jupiter at a distance of 80,967 miles (130,300 km) before heading for the edge of the Solar System. Space probes close to the Sun can use solar panels for power to operate and to communicate with Earth. For travel beyond Mars, electric generators need to be on board.

Pioneer 10 view of Jupiter

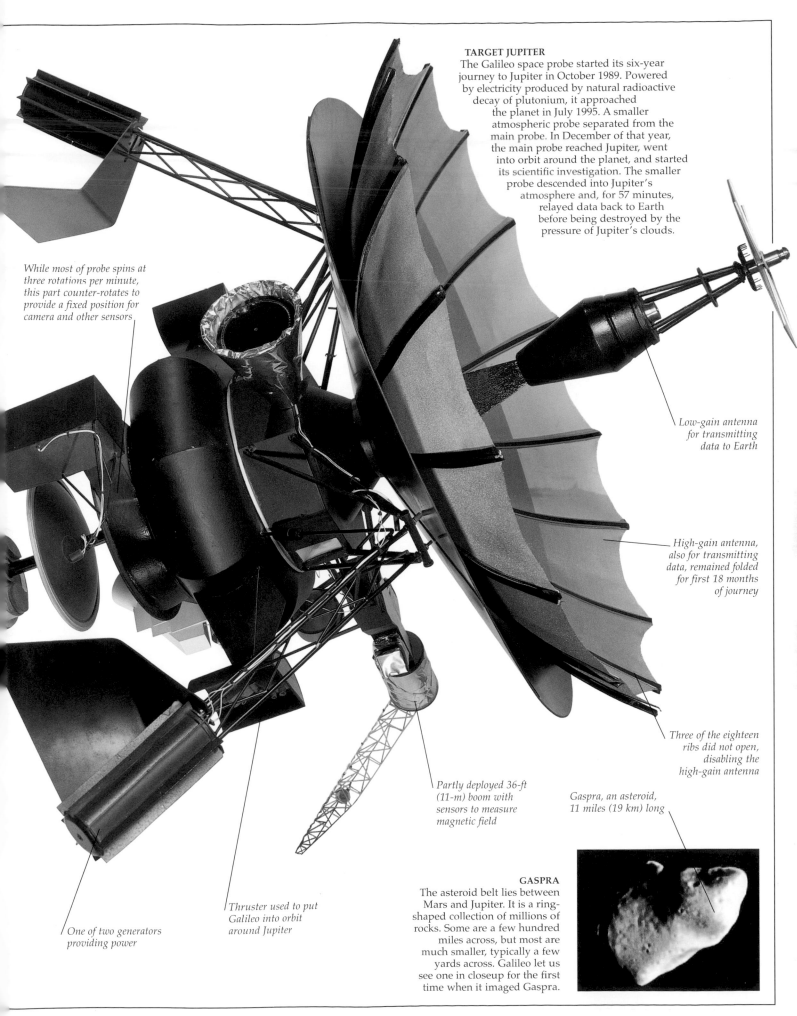

TARGET JUPITER

The Galileo space probe started its six-year journey to Jupiter in October 1989. Powered by electricity produced by natural radioactive decay of plutonium, it approached the planet in July 1995. A smaller atmospheric probe separated from the main probe. In December of that year, the main probe reached Jupiter, went into orbit around the planet, and started its scientific investigation. The smaller probe descended into Jupiter's atmosphere and, for 57 minutes, relayed data back to Earth before being destroyed by the pressure of Jupiter's clouds.

While most of probe spins at three rotations per minute, this part counter-rotates to provide a fixed position for camera and other sensors

Low-gain antenna for transmitting data to Earth

High-gain antenna, also for transmitting data, remained folded for first 18 months of journey

Three of the eighteen ribs did not open, disabling the high-gain antenna

Partly deployed 36-ft (11-m) boom with sensors to measure magnetic field

Gaspra, an asteroid, 11 miles (19 km) long

One of two generators providing power

Thruster used to put Galileo into orbit around Jupiter

GASPRA

The asteroid belt lies between Mars and Jupiter. It is a ring-shaped collection of millions of rocks. Some are a few hundred miles across, but most are much smaller, typically a few yards across. Galileo let us see one in closeup for the first time when it imaged Gaspra.

In-depth investigators

ON BOARD A SPACE PROBE are about 10 to 20 highly sensitive scientific instruments. These instruments record, monitor, and carry out experiments for Earth-based scientists. The information they supply enables astronomers and space scientists to build up a picture of the objects in space. The instruments are arguably the most important part of a space probe. However, the main structure must be able to transport, protect, and power them. Scientists often have to design instruments to work in unknown conditions and investigate objects previously viewed only from Earth. They may have to wait years before the instruments start to work and the results come in.

JOURNEY'S END
Space probes travel hundreds of millions of miles from Earth for years at a time. Most complete their journeys, but Mars-96, shown here, had a faulty booster rocket and failed to leave Earth orbit.

Cassini

Huygens   *Saturn*

SPACE PROBE TO SATURN
One of the most expensive and ambitious space probes to be built so far will reach Saturn in 2004 after a seven-year journey. Cassini will orbit the planet and its moons for four years. Huygens, a small probe, will be released to investigate the atmosphere and surface of Saturn's largest moon, Titan.

Giotto's cometlike Star of Bethlehem

Dish antenna for transmitting data and receiving instructions from Earth

Tank holds fuel for fine-control thrusters

Ten instruments on experiment platform

Electronic camera took images on close approach every four seconds

Bumper shield (not shown) fitted here. This side of Giotto approached comet

NAMING NAMES
ESA's probe to Halley's Comet in 1986 was called Giotto after the Italian painter Giotto di Bondone. His fresco *Adoration of the Magi*, completed around 1305, depicts a cometlike star. Halley's Comet had been in Earth's sky in 1301 and Giotto is thought to have used it as a model for his star.

TITAN
Titan is shrouded by a thick, orange, nitrogen-rich atmosphere. Scientists do not know what they'll find on Titan's surface. Huygens will land either in an oceanlike lake of liquid methane or on a dry surface. Its instruments are prepared for both and will provide results in either case.

Huygens model above Earth during drop-test

GIOTTO
Five probes traveled toward Halley's Comet in 1986. The most successful was ESA's Giotto. It got within 375 miles (600 km) of the comet's nucleus. The probe approached the comet at 149,133 mph (240,000 kmph) and before reaching the nucleus, traveled through a halo of gas and dust. It was the first probe ever to be protected by a bumper shield.

TESTING HUYGENS
A heat shield will protect Huygens as it drops through Titan's upper atmosphere. The shield will be ejected, and the instruments will test the lower atmosphere while parachutes ensure a slow descent to Titan's surface. A full-size model was drop-tested to make sure everything works in sequence.

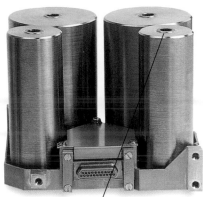

HOW COLD?
This instrument on board Huygens will measure the temperature of gases as the probe descends through Titan's atmosphere, and liquids as it lands on its surface. The instrument will also measure how easily the gases and liquids transmit heat.

Gas or liquid flows through holes

DENSITY
If the Huygens probe lands in liquid on Titan's surface, the level at which this instrument floats will indicate the liquid's density. It will tell us whether it is water or a thicker liquid.

FIRST TOUCH
This is the part of Huygens that is expected to hit the surface of Titan first. It can measure how quickly the probe stops and whether it has hit land or ocean. If it hits land, it can tell the difference between rock, soil, and ice. If it hits ocean, another instrument (left) will measure the density of the liquid.

Transmitter receives and sends "beeps"

Cable transfers data for storage then transmission

COMPOSITION CRACKER
These two pieces of Huygens equipment, speakers and receivers combined, measure how fast a "beep" sound travels from one to the other. The results help determine the density, temperature, and composition of Titan's atmosphere and surface.

Temperature and density instruments inside

Composition cracker

This part will touch Titan first

TOP HAT SCIENCE
The five experiments featured here were fitted together in this one piece of equipment known as the Surface Science Package (SSP). It is about the size and shape of a top hat. The SSP and five more experiments were all thoroughly tested before being fitted onto Huygens about a year before launch. International teams of scientists worked on the experiments. The SSP was prepared by a team from Canterbury, England.

First touch

Surface Science Package

Ocean deep

Composition cracker

DESCENT TO TITAN
In this artist's impression, Huygens is falling through Titan's atmosphere. It will transmit data for about 2.5 hours as it falls and when it lands.

STAY COOL
Space technicians work on Huygens at facilities in Bordeaux, France. They are fitting the heat shield that will protect Huygens against high temperatures. Huygens will be submitted to temperatures about 3,290 °F (1,800 °C) to 3,600 °F (2,000 °C), but its internal temperature must not exceed 350 °F (180 °C).

OCEAN DEEP
The sonar system used by submarines on Earth will be used in space for the first time on Huygens. If Huygens lands in an ocean, it will transmit sound that will reflect off the ocean bed. Measure of the time taken for this sound to echo will indicate ocean depth.

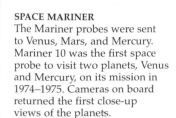

SPACE MARINER
The Mariner probes were sent to Venus, Mars, and Mercury. Mariner 10 was the first space probe to visit two planets, Venus and Mercury, on its mission in 1974–1975. Cameras on board returned the first close-up views of the planets.

Landers and discoverers

SPACE PROBES ARE OUR EYES in space and much more besides. Since the day they gave us our first detailed look at the Moon, they have made hundreds of thousands of images for us. They have shown us Mercury's cratered terrain, the red deserts of Mars, and the mountains and plains beneath the Venusian clouds. They have tested thick, hostile atmospheres, returned moon rock to Earth, and searched Martian dust for signs of life. Probes follow preprogrammed instructions to look and test information already gathered. They make discoveries that are expected, but also some that are not. Much of our knowledge about the Solar System in the second half of the 20th century has come from using probes, and the success of these space discoverers and landers means future missions are guaranteed.

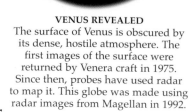

VENUS REVEALED
The surface of Venus is obscured by its dense, hostile atmosphere. The first images of the surface were returned by Venera craft in 1975. Since then, probes have used radar to map it. This globe was made using radar images from Magellan in 1992.

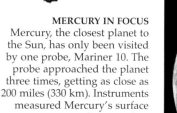

MERCURY IN FOCUS
Mercury, the closest planet to the Sun, has only been visited by one probe, Mariner 10. The probe approached the planet three times, getting as close as 200 miles (330 km). Instruments measured Mercury's surface temperature, discovered its magnetic field, and made more than 10,000 images. The best of the images were fitted together to produce a detailed view of this dry, lifeless planet.

FAR SIDE OF THE MOON
For centuries, the Moon has been studied from Earth. Starting in 1959, both U.S. and Soviet probes have visited it. The early observations were of the same side, the one always facing Earth. The far side of the Moon was first imaged by a Soviet probe on October 4, 1959.

LUNOKHOD EXPLORER
The first of two Soviet robotic lunar explorers landed on the Moon on November 17, 1970. The eight-wheeled Earth-controlled Lunokhod 1 worked on the lunar surface for 10 months, covering 6 miles (10 km) as it made images and tested the surface. Lunokhod 2 traveled 23 miles (37 km) as it explored a different part of the Moon in 1973.

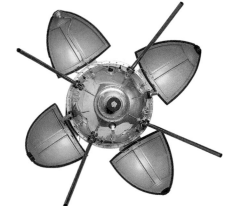

MOON DETECTIVES
The Soviet Luna series of space probes studied the Moon for almost 20 years. They were the first probes to travel to the Moon, to image the far side, to crash-land on it, and to orbit it. Luna 9 successfully achieved the first soft landing on January 31, 1966, and made the first panoramic pictures of the lunar surface, which showed details only 1 mm across.

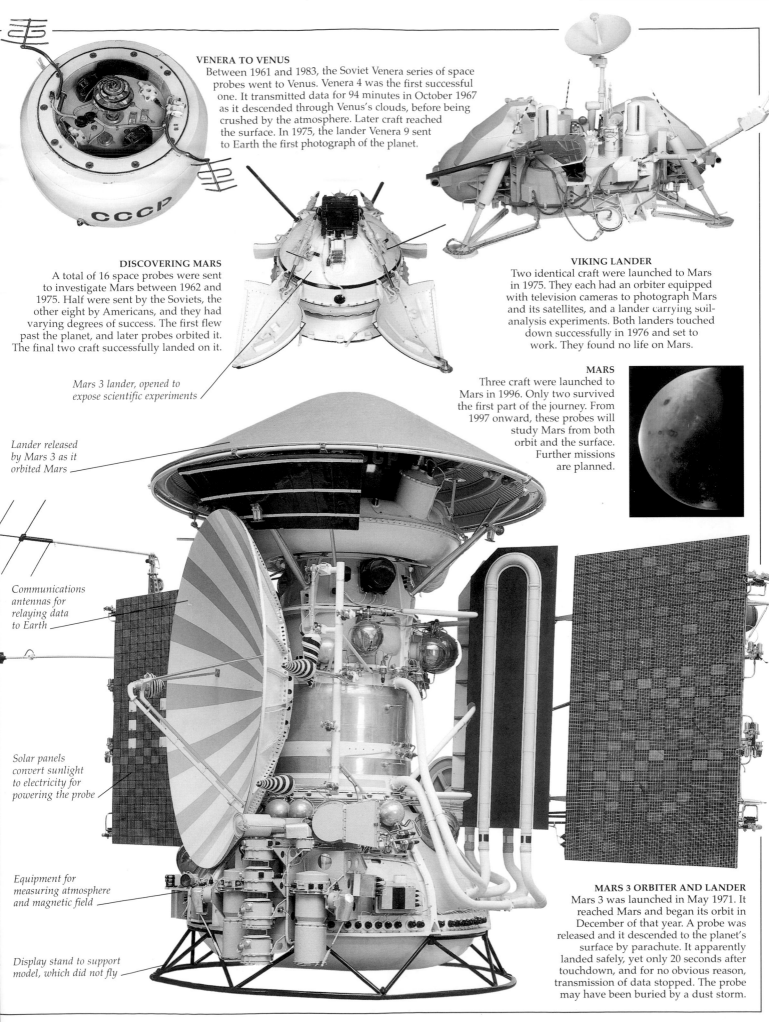

VENERA TO VENUS
Between 1961 and 1983, the Soviet Venera series of space probes went to Venus. Venera 4 was the first successful one. It transmitted data for 94 minutes in October 1967 as it descended through Venus's clouds, before being crushed by the atmosphere. Later craft reached the surface. In 1975, the lander Venera 9 sent to Earth the first photograph of the planet.

DISCOVERING MARS
A total of 16 space probes were sent to investigate Mars between 1962 and 1975. Half were sent by the Soviets, the other eight by Americans, and they had varying degrees of success. The first flew past the planet, and later probes orbited it. The final two craft successfully landed on it.

Mars 3 lander, opened to expose scientific experiments

Lander released by Mars 3 as it orbited Mars

VIKING LANDER
Two identical craft were launched to Mars in 1975. They each had an orbiter equipped with television cameras to photograph Mars and its satellites, and a lander carrying soil-analysis experiments. Both landers touched down successfully in 1976 and set to work. They found no life on Mars.

MARS
Three craft were launched to Mars in 1996. Only two survived the first part of the journey. From 1997 onward, these probes will study Mars from both orbit and the surface. Further missions are planned.

Communications antennas for relaying data to Earth

Solar panels convert sunlight to electricity for powering the probe

Equipment for measuring atmosphere and magnetic field

Display stand to support model, which did not fly

MARS 3 ORBITER AND LANDER
Mars 3 was launched in May 1971. It reached Mars and began its orbit in December of that year. A probe was released and it descended to the planet's surface by parachute. It apparently landed safely, yet only 20 seconds after touchdown, and for no obvious reason, transmission of data stopped. The probe may have been buried by a dust storm.

Crowded space

THE MOON IS EARTH'S ONLY NATURAL SATELLITE and its closest neighbor in space. In between the two is the virtual vacuum of space itself. But anyone visiting Earth for the first time might think that the volume of space immediately around Earth is crowded. Within a few thousand miles of its surface, there are about a thousand operational satellites. Each one is a specialized scientific instrument following its own path around Earth. The satellites work for us in a variety of ways. Perhaps the most important are the telecommunication satellites that affect the lives of most of us. They give us global communication at the touch of a button, they beam television pictures to our living rooms, and are used in all types of business, day and night.

TELSTAR
The first transatlantic live television pictures were transmitted in July 1962 by Telstar, a round, 35-in (90-cm) wide satellite covered in solar cells. In the years that followed, live television became an increasing part of everyday life. By 1987, Roman Catholics on five continents could join Pope John Paul II in a live broadcast using 23 satellites.

Pocket-sized navigation systems can pinpoint your position to within 49 ft (15 m)

NAVIGATION
Aircraft pilots, yachtsmen, soldiers, and now hikers navigate their way about Earth using satellites. The Global Positioning System (GPS) uses a set of 24 satellites in orbit around Earth. The user sends a signal from a hand set, like this one, which is received by up to 12 of the satellites. Return data give location, direction, and speed.

Terrorist at Munich Olympic Games

"Live Aid" concert finale

GOOD NEWS, BAD NEWS
Satellites can turn once-local events into global occasions. In 1964, Tokyo's opening ceremony of the Olympic Games was transmitted around the world. However by 1972, at the Munich Games, terrorists had learned that live pictures could draw attention to their cause. In 1985, satellite television broadcast "Live Aid" to 2 billion people worldwide.

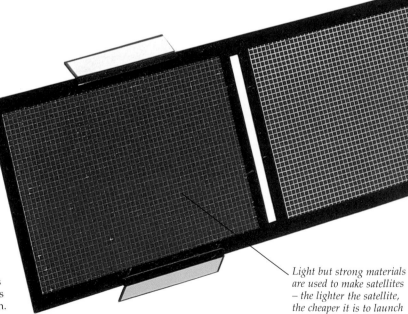

Light but strong materials are used to make satellites – the lighter the satellite, the cheaper it is to launch

BUSY LINES
A telecommunications satellite has to handle tens of thousands of phone calls, television signals, and other electronic links at once. The first satellite to relay signals from one ground station to another was Telstar, launched by the U.S. in 1962. Other areas of the world developed their own systems. Nations across Europe use the European Communications Satellite (ECS). Global entities, such as Intelsat, now provide links among the systems. A series of satellites working together as they circle the world is known as a constellation.

GROUND CONTROL
Most satellites are launched by rocket, but some are taken into space in the payload bay of a space shuttle. Once the satellite has separated from the launcher, an on-board motor propels it into its correct orbit. Smaller maneuvers are made by the satellite's propulsion system throughout its lifetime to maintain its correct position in space. The rocket launch center hands over control to the satellite control center. It uses ground stations, like this one in Belgium, to track the satellite, receive its signals, monitor its health, and send commands.

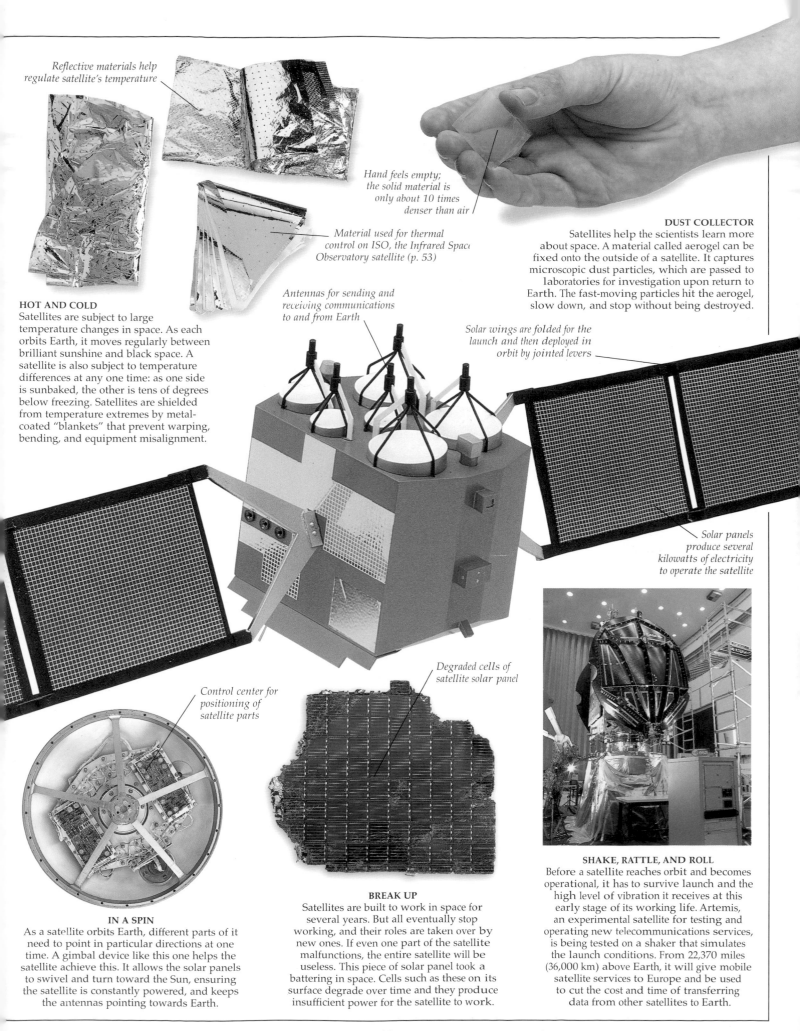

Reflective materials help regulate satellite's temperature

Hand feels empty; the solid material is only about 10 times denser than air

Material used for thermal control on ISO, the Infrared Space Observatory satellite (p. 53)

HOT AND COLD
Satellites are subject to large temperature changes in space. As each orbits Earth, it moves regularly between brilliant sunshine and black space. A satellite is also subject to temperature differences at any one time: as one side is sunbaked, the other is tens of degrees below freezing. Satellites are shielded from temperature extremes by metal-coated "blankets" that prevent warping, bending, and equipment misalignment.

DUST COLLECTOR
Satellites help the scientists learn more about space. A material called aerogel can be fixed onto the outside of a satellite. It captures microscopic dust particles, which are passed to laboratories for investigation upon return to Earth. The fast-moving particles hit the aerogel, slow down, and stop without being destroyed.

Antennas for sending and receiving communications to and from Earth

Solar wings are folded for the launch and then deployed in orbit by jointed levers

Solar panels produce several kilowatts of electricity to operate the satellite

Control center for positioning of satellite parts

Degraded cells of satellite solar panel

IN A SPIN
As a satellite orbits Earth, different parts of it need to point in particular directions at one time. A gimbal device like this one helps the satellite achieve this. It allows the solar panels to swivel and turn toward the Sun, ensuring the satellite is constantly powered, and keeps the antennas pointing towards Earth.

BREAK UP
Satellites are built to work in space for several years. But all eventually stop working, and their roles are taken over by new ones. If even one part of the satellite malfunctions, the entire satellite will be useless. This piece of solar panel took a battering in space. Cells such as these on its surface degrade over time and they produce insufficient power for the satellite to work.

SHAKE, RATTLE, AND ROLL
Before a satellite reaches orbit and becomes operational, it has to survive launch and the high level of vibration it receives at this early stage of its working life. Artemis, an experimental satellite for testing and operating new telecommunications services, is being tested on a shaker that simulates the launch conditions. From 22,370 miles (36,000 km) above Earth, it will give mobile satellite services to Europe and be used to cut the cost and time of transferring data from other satellites to Earth.

Looking at Earth

SATELLITES ARE TAKING A CLOSE LOOK at our planet. In their different orbits around the Earth, they can survey the whole globe repeatedly or stay over one spot. Each concentrates on collecting a specific type of information. Weather satellites look at clouds and study the Earth's atmosphere or record the planet's range of surface temperatures. Others map artificial structures and natural resources such as water, soil and minerals, and flora and fauna. Ocean currents, ice movement, and animals and birds are followed. By taking time-lapse images of Earth, satellites are making records of short- and long-term planetary changes. The information they collect can be used to predict changes and to avoid problems like soil erosion and floods.

MAN-MADE DISASTER
The Landsat 5 satellite gave us a bird's-eye view of a vast oil slick on the Saudi Arabian shoreline in 1991. False colors have been added to the image. The slick is colored rusty red. The oil had been deliberately released one month earlier by Iraqi soldiers in Kuwait.

FOUR CORNERS
The European Remote Sensing (ERS) series of satellites started work in 1991. ERS-1 returned several thousand pages worth of information every second. ERS-1 made these four views of parts of Europe (above and in other corners) in 1992. Its successor, ERS-2, was launched in 1995. It charts the world's ozone layer every three days.

Paris

London

BIRD-SPOTTING
The fish-eating Steller's sea eagle breeds in Siberia. As winter approaches, the sea starts to freeze and the eagle's supply of food is cut off. Satellite tracking follows the birds as they fly south to spend the winter on the Japanese island of Hokkaido.

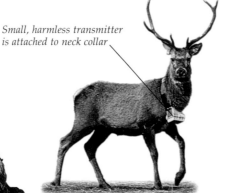

Small, harmless transmitter is attached to neck collar

DEERSTALKER
Small transmitters are attached to animals, like this red deer. As the deer moves about, a signal is released, which is picked up by satellite. Over time, its habitual movements are revealed. By knowing where animals breed, feed, and spend winter, conservationists can try to protect such sites and so conserve the creatures.

City of Detroit

Geometrically shaped man-made fields stand out

EYE IN THE SKY
France's Earth observation satellite, Spot-1, was launched in 1986. Every 26 days, it photographed the whole of Earth's surface. On board were two telescopes, each aimed at the Earth and observing a strip of land 37 miles (60 km) wide. Objects only 33 ft (10 m) across were recorded. This Spot-1 picture of farmland in Canada was made in July 1988. False colors identify different crops at different stages of growth. Lake St. Clair is at the top of the picture and Lake Erie at the bottom, both shown in green.

MAN ON THE MOVE

Air-, sea-, and land-based military all use satellite systems. Their planes and ships are equipped with navigation systems. For the single soldier in remote terrain, such as desert, a navigation backpack is the answer. It will tell him where he is and in which direction to move. A portable communications system keeps him in touch with other troops.

Portable folding satellite dish

Vienna

Solar cells supply energy for Meteosat to function

Upper platform carries communication equipment

WEATHER WATCH

Meteosat satellites have been in operation since 1977. Weather satellites such as Meteosat are in geostationary orbit: they orbit at the same speed that the Earth turns, so they stay above a particular spot on Earth and monitor the same region at all times. Data from these and other satellites are combined to study global weather patterns and used to make daily forecasts.

ERUPTION

Images of natural phenomena, such as volcanoes, are made by satellites and by astronaut-operated equipment aboard the space shuttle and Mir. Smoke and ash from an active volcano can be monitored, and aircraft warned away. Ground movements of a few inches or feet may warn of a volcanic eruption. Such small movements can be detected and the alarm raised.

LOOK AND LEARN

Events and places on Earth can be watched by people thousands of miles away because of communication satellites. People can learn about other nations and cultures from their own homes. In 1975, over 2,400 villages in India were given satellite dishes and television sets. Direct broadcasting by satellite instructed them on hygiene and health, family planning, and farming methods.

Zeeland, the Netherlands

Looking into space

SCIENTIFIC SATELLITES ARE USED BY ASTRONOMERS to look away from Earth and into space. These telescopes collect and record data in much the same way that telescopes do on Earth. But from their vantage point, they can study the Universe 24 hours a day, 365 days a year. Space telescopes operate in a range of wavelengths. Much of the information they collect, such as that at X-ray wavelengths, would be stopped from reaching ground-based instruments by Earth's atmosphere. Data collected by telescopes working in optical, X-ray, infrared, ultraviolet, microwave, and other wavelengths are combined to create a more complete view of space.

This composite "picture" is collected, stored, and sent to a ground station, where it is decoded by computers. Astronomers all over the world have been looking at the Universe in this way for about 30 years.

EARLY ASTRONOMY
Astronomers once recorded their findings in drawings, like this one. Today, electronic devices record data transmitted from telescopes in orbit around Earth.

Plane of Milky Way

MIRROR IMAGES
Tremendous amounts of energy are needed to create X-rays, so wherever they are detected, there is violent activity. The Advanced X-ray Astrophysics Facility (AXAF) is to be the next X-ray space telescope to image and study X-ray sources. Once released by the space shuttle in 1998, it will propel itself to its higher orbit and start to work using its four pairs of mirrors.

OUR GALACTIC CENTER
The High Energy Astrophysics Observatory X-ray satellite telescope took this false-color X-ray view of our galaxy. It covers two-thirds of Earth's sky. The plane of the Milky Way crosses the center of the picture from left to right. The black, then red, areas are the most intense X-ray emitters. The yellow and green areas emit less, and the blue emits the least X-ray energy.

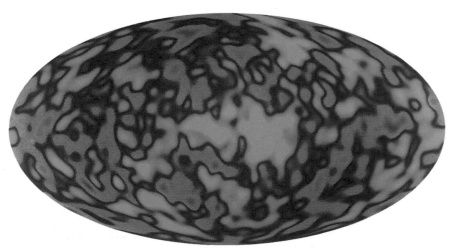

RIPPLES IN THE SKY
In 1992, the Cosmic Background Explorer (COBE) satellite discovered slight temperature differences in the Universe's microwave background radiation. In this false-color microwave map of the whole sky, the average temperature of the background radiation is shown as deep blue. The pink and red areas are warmer, and the pale blue is cooler. These were the ripples scientists predicted should exist in background radiation created by the Big Bang.

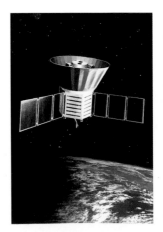

MICROWAVE IMAGES
The first satellite telescope to look at space in the microwave region was launched by rocket into an orbit about 570 miles (917 km) above Earth. COBE started work in late 1989. It provided the first observational proof for the theory that the Universe was created about 15 billion years ago in a huge explosion we call the Big Bang.

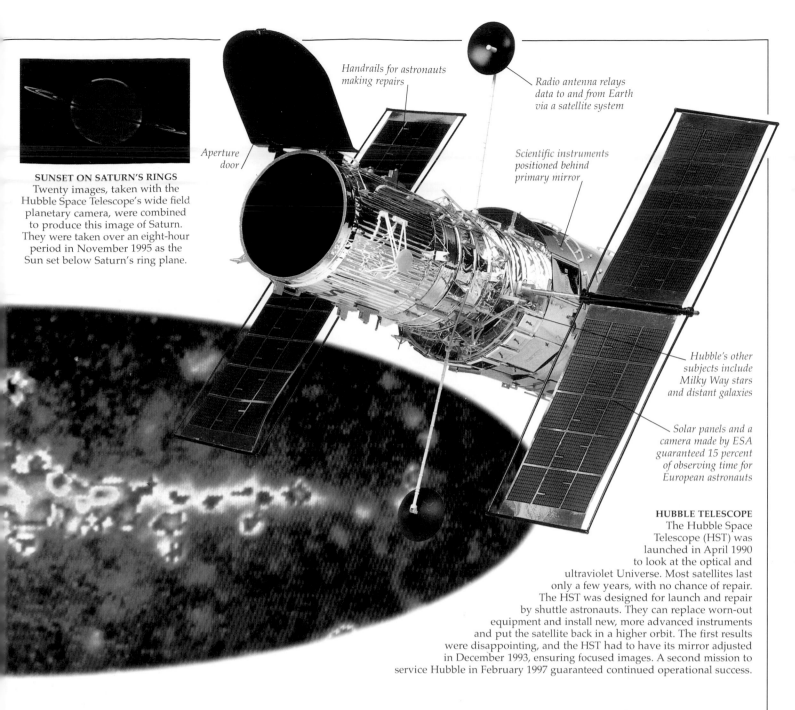

SUNSET ON SATURN'S RINGS
Twenty images, taken with the Hubble Space Telescope's wide field planetary camera, were combined to produce this image of Saturn. They were taken over an eight-hour period in November 1995 as the Sun set below Saturn's ring plane.

Handrails for astronauts making repairs

Radio antenna relays data to and from Earth via a satellite system

Aperture door

Scientific instruments positioned behind primary mirror

Hubble's other subjects include Milky Way stars and distant galaxies

Solar panels and a camera made by ESA guaranteed 15 percent of observing time for European astronauts

HUBBLE TELESCOPE
The Hubble Space Telescope (HST) was launched in April 1990 to look at the optical and ultraviolet Universe. Most satellites last only a few years, with no chance of repair. The HST was designed for launch and repair by shuttle astronauts. They can replace worn-out equipment and install new, more advanced instruments and put the satellite back in a higher orbit. The first results were disappointing, and the HST had to have its mirror adjusted in December 1993, ensuring focused images. A second mission to service Hubble in February 1997 guaranteed continued operational success.

ISO being tested by ESA

Launch of ISO by Ariane on November 4, 1995

Impression of ISO in orbit

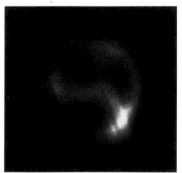

Picture taken by ISO of supernova, an exploding star

INFRARED OBSERVATIONS
The Infrared Space Observatory (ISO), the largest and most complex scientific satellite to be launched by the European Space Agency, started work in late 1995. From its elliptical orbit, which takes it from 600 to 43,000 miles (1,000 to 70,000 km) above the Earth, ISO uses its two-foot (60-cm) mirror to observe the near and distant Universe, making on average 45 observations a day. Data on Saturn, star births, colliding galaxies, and water ice in our galaxy have all been sent to ESA's tracking station in Madrid.

The future in space

SPACE TRAVEL IS GOING to be as familiar in the years ahead as air travel became in the 20th century. It will involve men, women, and children traveling more often and making longer trips. People will once again be on the Moon's surface, and the first astronauts will walk on Mars. Travelers will have the choice of going as a tourist for a short stay in a hotel, or in the more distant future setting up home in a Moon or Mars base. Astronauts will continue to explore and work from space stations. They will be joined by a new breed of robotic space workers operating telescopes and mining equipment on the Moon. These ideas are being considered or planned by space agencies and businesses right now in the U.S., Canada, Europe, and Japan.

Satellite dish

HOLIDAY RESORT
Japanese businessmen are planning an Earth-orbiting hotel, shown above, followed by one on the Moon. The hotel is built around a 787-ft (240-m) elevator shaft. The guest rooms are on a wheel that turns three times a minute. It will be a base for spacewalks, sightseeing tours to the Moon, and unique sports and games in weightlessness.

Command module

Space shuttle

SPACE FOR EVERYONE
The cost of launching into space is currently very high. Space tourists need a new reusable vehicle that runs cheaply and frequently, one that could be used for straightforward space flights, for special occasions such as a space wedding, and for docking with an orbiting hotel. From Earth spaceport to orbiting hotel would take an hour.

FISHY BUSINESS
New ways of providing food are needed if long-term space trips are to be a reality. At present, astronauts take their food with them or have stocks replenished by visiting crews. Japanese crews are fond of eating fresh fish and wish to farm fish in space to produce sushi. To this end, these nonedible "trial" fish have mated and produced young in space.

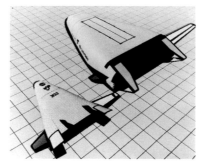

SPACE PLANE
$1 billion is being spent on developing the space plane replacement for the space shuttle. The first half-scale model, X-33 (far left), will not have a crew. The full-scale version, to be known as VentureStar, will have a crew. Its triangular body will be of light materials, it will have fins instead of wings, and all parts will be reusable.

Lunar rover

SPACE PLAY
The space scientists, engineers, and astronauts of the near future are children today. These cardboard toys came free with McDonald's Happy Meals in the US in 1991, and were free McDonald's give aways in Germany in 1993. They were produced in collaboration with the Young Astronaut Council, which encourages children in America to learn about science, math, and space.

ROBOT TRAVELER
Unmanned craft will continue to be used to explore our space neighborhood. Space probes will fly by, and orbit, the planets and their moons. Landers will return with Martian and asteroid rock, and with dusty snow from the heart of a comet. Robots will work on space stations. Those at Moon or Mars bases will be designed to encounter lunar and planetary surfaces.

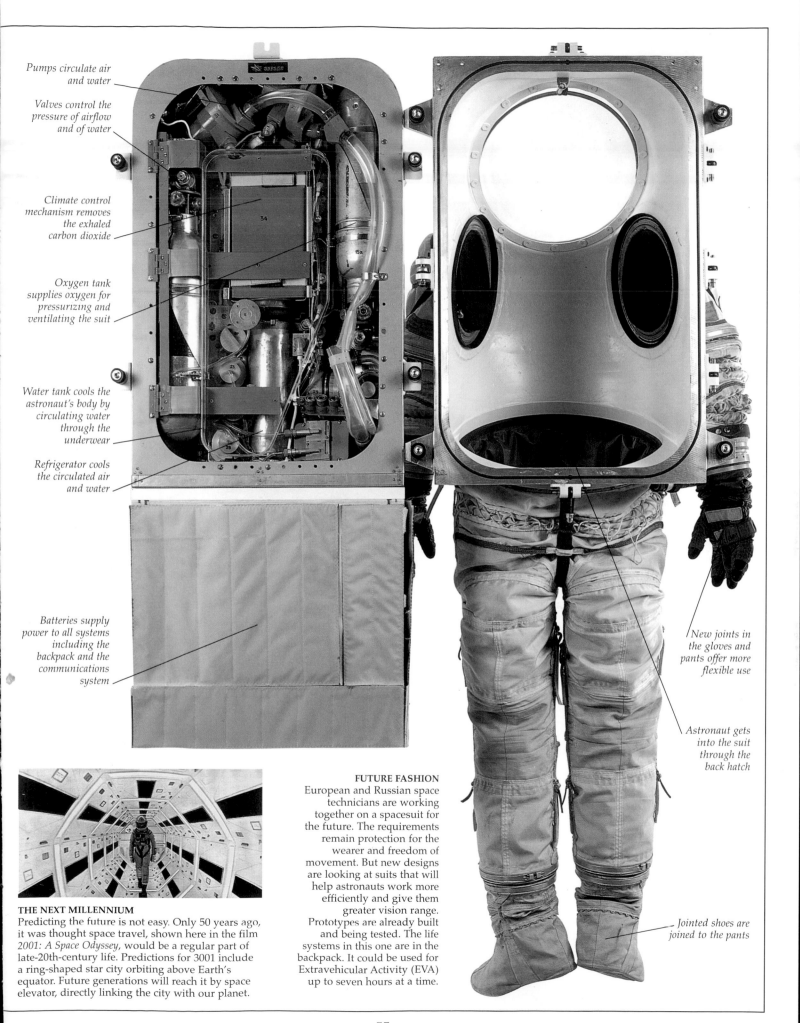

Pumps circulate air and water

Valves control the pressure of airflow and of water

Climate control mechanism removes the exhaled carbon dioxide

Oxygen tank supplies oxygen for pressurizing and ventilating the suit

Water tank cools the astronaut's body by circulating water through the underwear

Refrigerator cools the circulated air and water

Batteries supply power to all systems including the backpack and the communications system

New joints in the gloves and pants offer more flexible use

Astronaut gets into the suit through the back hatch

Jointed shoes are joined to the pants

THE NEXT MILLENNIUM
Predicting the future is not easy. Only 50 years ago, it was thought space travel, shown here in the film *2001: A Space Odyssey,* would be a regular part of late-20th-century life. Predictions for 3001 include a ring-shaped star city orbiting above Earth's equator. Future generations will reach it by space elevator, directly linking the city with our planet.

FUTURE FASHION
European and Russian space technicians are working together on a spacesuit for the future. The requirements remain protection for the wearer and freedom of movement. But new designs are looking at suits that will help astronauts work more efficiently and give them greater vision range. Prototypes are already built and being tested. The life systems in this one are in the backpack. It could be used for Extravehicular Activity (EVA) up to seven hours at a time.

Space technology on Earth

Space INDUSTRY RESEARCH is used to benefit our everyday lives. Technologies and techniques designed for use in space have been transferred to or adapted for life on Earth, often in fields totally unrelated to the original research. An everyday item such as food wrapping was developed from reflective film used on satellites. Car-control systems used by one-handed drivers came from the one-handed technique used in the Lunar Rover. Modern smoke-detection systems use technology developed for smoke detection on the Skylab space station. Tens of thousands of spin-offs have come from space research, many of them have been adapted for medicine.

LASER-BEAM SPEECH
Robot and laser technology is used in equipment for people with disabilities. The boy above, who is unable to speak, is wearing a headpiece with laser equipment. By using the laser to operate a voice synthesizer, he is able to communicate.

INSULIN PUMP
Robert Fischell, American space scientist, invented an insulin pump for diabetics. Once implanted in the body, the device automatically delivers precise preprogrammed amounts of insulin. The pumping mechanism is based on technology used by the Viking craft that landed on the planet Mars.

KEEPING CLEAN
An industrial cleaning method that is quick, easy to use, and harmless to the environment has grown out of space research. Ricelike pellets of dry ice (solid carbon dioxide) are blasted at supersonic speeds to remove surface dirt. On impact, the ice turns to gas, the dirt falls away, and the underlying material is unharmed.

Artificial hand and control system

SPACE ON THE SLOPES
Protective clothing designed for astronauts is now used on the ski slopes. The Apollo helmet design, which gave the astronauts fog-free sight, has been adapted for use in ski goggles. Electrically heated or fan-controlled goggles keep moisture from condensing inside, and the goggles from fogging up.

Mercury astronauts

THE SPACE "LOOK"
The first U.S. astronauts, on the Mercury rockets, wore silver suits designed to reflect heat. The space look was transferred to haute couture when French fashion designer André Courrèges produced his "space age" collection in 1964. Within months, off-the-rack space-influenced fashions were available to everyone.

Silver kidskin outfit including cap with visor

HAND CONTROL
The micro-miniaturization of parts for space has been adapted for use on Earth. Artificial limbs with controls as small as coins have been developed. This makes the limbs lighter and easier to use. Devices no larger than a pinhead are placed in a human heart to monitor its rhythm; such tiny instruments are developed from space technology.

Patient enters body scanner to have body imaged

SHARP VIEW
An image-enhancement technique devised to improve the sharpness of Moon photographs is used in medical photography. It gives doctors a better basis for diagnosis by providing more accurate images. This MRI scan gives a clear overall view of what is happening inside the human body.

BAR CODE SCANNING
A trip to the supermarket means an encounter with space technology – from the food you buy to the scanner that reads bar codes to register the prices. Many of the ready-to-eat and dried meals introduced in the 1980s and 1990s are the result of space research.

BRACE YOURSELF
A metal alloy of nickel and titanium called nitinol is used in teeth braces. Nitinol was originally developed for space equipment such as antennas. The antennas are compacted for launch; they are expanded to full size in space. Nitinol was the ideal material for the job as it has the ability to return to its original shape after bending. Back on Earth, nitinol allows braces to exert continuous pull on teeth. This reduces the number of brace changes needed as the teeth are pulled into shape.

Nitinol arch wires held in place by colored fittings apply pressure to straighten teeth

Image shows inside and outside of hand at the same time

False color is added to make features stand out

Kidney dialysis machine removes waste materials from the patient's blood

HUMAN HAND MAP
Techniques developed to enhance satellite images of the Earth have been used to make maps of the human body for medical purposes. In this computer image of a hand with fingers extended, the contour of each finger shows the shape of the hand. At the same time the structure of the bones underneath is revealed.

Digital display

HELPING HAND FOR HOSPITALS
Many of the results of space research are found in hospitals around the world. For example, reflective blankets used to retain an accident victim's body heat, kidney dialysis machines for purifying blood, special beds for burn patients, and miniaturized television cameras worn on a surgeon's head to allow others to watch and learn from an operation have all been developed from space technology.

TIME UNDER PRESSURE
Space spin-offs are everywhere in daily life. Watches have digital displays and glass capable of surviving increased gravitational force. Clothes are made with lightweight, thermal fabrics, qualities essential for space materials. Athletic footwear has stay-dry insoles, and sports helmets and shin guards are lined with shock-absorbing foam.

What lies ahead

SPACE SCIENTISTS have already taken the first firm steps in planning for our near future in space. They are using the knowledge of space, and how humans can live and work in it, that was acquired through years of research. The space race has been replaced by a new spirit of international cooperation as nations that once worked alone join together to build a space station for the benefit of all. As people continue to benefit from space technology, more efficient satellites are being built and launched into service. About 500 satellites are currently in preparation to replace those already in space as they become outmoded.

ALPHA
The United States, Canada, Russia, Japan, and the European Space Agency (ESA) are working together to build the Alpha space station. This computer-generated image shows how it will look in space.

UNDER CONSTRUCTION
Each contributor to Alpha is responsible for building different parts. The Russians are constructing a service module that is 43 ft (13 m) long. It will serve as a living area and laboratory for a crew of three in the early stages of Alpha.

Columbus

Space plane docks with Columbus in orbit

SPACE LABORATORY
The European Space Agency (ESA)'s contribution to Alpha is a space laboratory called Columbus. Scientists around the world have already been asked for their experiment proposals. ESA is also working on a supply vehicle for the station and a separate vehicle, or space plane, to transfer the space station astronauts.

ariane 5

esa   *esa*

OXYGEN PRODUCTION
Research into life support systems required this scientist to spend 15 days in a sealed chamber with 30,000 wheat plants. The aim was to prove that plants can provide enough oxygen for astronauts on long trips. The scientist breathed the oxygen given off by the wheat, which in turn used the carbon dioxide he breathed out.

Central strut supports solar cells and radiators

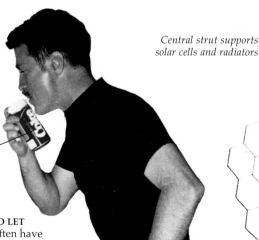

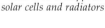

Coca-Cola and Pepsi both provided drinks for space shuttle Challenger in 1985

SPACE TO LET
Earth-based events often have commercial sponsors who provide financial backing in exchange for publicity for their company or product. Companies are now venturing into space. A Japanese television company has sponsored an astronaut, and an Austrian beverage firm has sponsored a flight to Mir.

Ariane 5 rocket launches space plane

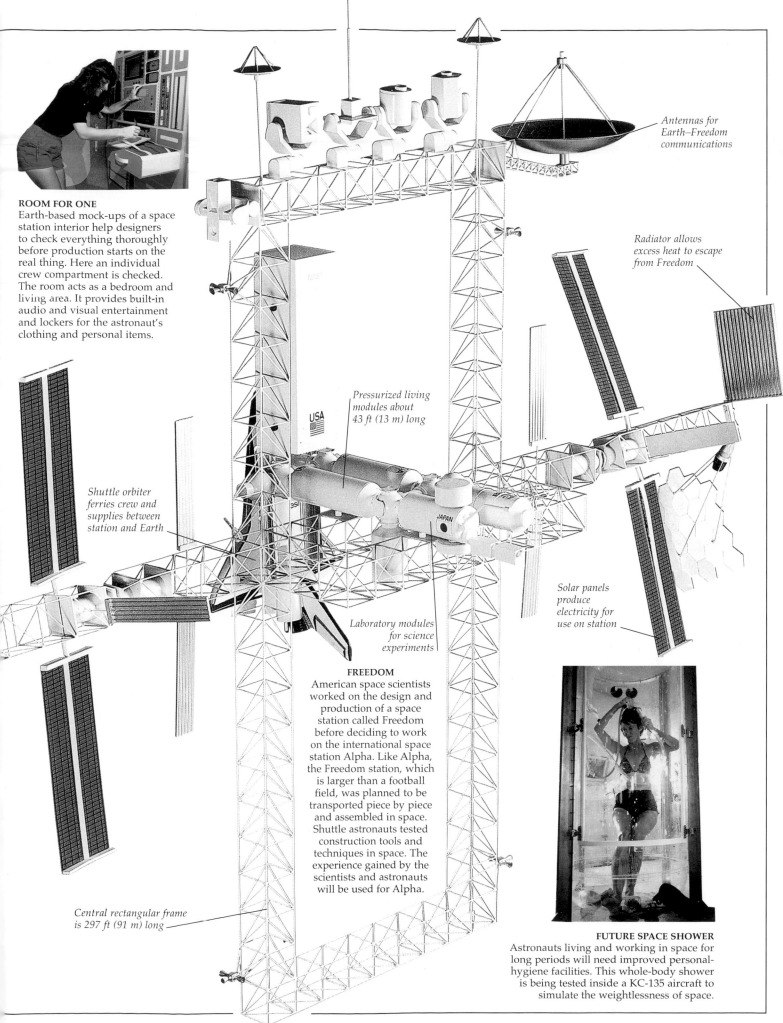

ROOM FOR ONE
Earth-based mock-ups of a space station interior help designers to check everything thoroughly before production starts on the real thing. Here an individual crew compartment is checked. The room acts as a bedroom and living area. It provides built-in audio and visual entertainment and lockers for the astronaut's clothing and personal items.

Antennas for Earth–Freedom communications

Radiator allows excess heat to escape from Freedom

Pressurized living modules about 43 ft (13 m) long

USA

JAPAN

Shuttle orbiter ferries crew and supplies between station and Earth

Solar panels produce electricity for use on station

Laboratory modules for science experiments

FREEDOM
American space scientists worked on the design and production of a space station called Freedom before deciding to work on the international space station Alpha. Like Alpha, the Freedom station, which is larger than a football field, was planned to be transported piece by piece and assembled in space. Shuttle astronauts tested construction tools and techniques in space. The experience gained by the scientists and astronauts will be used for Alpha.

Central rectangular frame is 297 ft (91 m) long

FUTURE SPACE SHOWER
Astronauts living and working in space for long periods will need improved personal-hygiene facilities. This whole-body shower is being tested inside a KC-135 aircraft to simulate the weightlessness of space.

Index

Acknowledgments

Dorling Kindersley would like to thank:
Heidi Graf and Birgit Schröder of the European Space Research and Technology Centre (ESTEC), Noordwijk, the Netherlands for their invaluable assistance; Alain Gonfalone; Hugo Marée, Philippe Ledent, Chantal Rolland, and Massimiliano Piergentili of the Euro Space Center, Transinne, Belgium (managed by CISET International); Helen Sharman; Neville Kidger; Dr. John Zarnecki and JRC Garry of the University of Kent; MK Herbert, Ray Merchant; Dr. David Hughes, Dr. Hugo Alleyne, and Dr. Simon Walker of The University of Sheffield; Prof. John Parkinson of Sheffield Hallam University; Amalgam Modelmakers and Designers; Nicholas Booth; J Thompson, Orthodontic Appliances; Hideo Imammura of the Shimizu Corporation, Tokyo, Japan; Dr. Martyn Gorman of the University of Aberdeen; Dr. Peter Reynolds; Prof. Kenichi Ijiri; Dr. Thais Russomano and Simon Evetts of King's College London; Clive Simpson; Karen Jefferson and Elena Mirskaya of Dorling Kindersley, Moscow Office.

Design and editorial assistance: Darren Troughton, Carey Scott, Nicki Waine

Additional research: Sean Stancioff

Additional photography: Geoff Brightling

Photographic assistance: Sarah Ashun

Additional modelmaking: Peter Minister, Milton Scott-Baron

Endpapers: Anna Martin

Index: Chris Bernstein

Picture credits
Dorling Kindersley would like to thank:

Moscow Museum, The Science Museum and The US Space and Rocket Centre, Alabama.
Photographs by: Stephen Oliver, close-up shot 21t; James Stevenson; Bob Gathney.

The publisher would like to thank the following for their kind permission to reproduce their photographs:

(t = top, c = center, a = above, b = below, l = left, r = right)

BOC Gases, Guildford: 56cla.
Bridgeman Art Library, London/New York: Adoration of the Magi, c.1305 by Giotto, Ambrogio Bondone (c.1266-1337) Scrovgeni (Arena) Chapel, Padua.
Casio Electronics Co. Ltd.: 57br.

Bruce Coleman: Robert P. Carr 35clb.
CLRC: 45c.
Corbis UK: 56bl; Corbis-Bettman-UPI 19cra, 21bl, 48cr.
ESA: 17bl, 30bc, 31c, 33br, 36-37, 37tr, 40tr, 41cr, 44br, 45bl, 45cb, 49c, 50tl, 50bl, 51tr, 51crb, 51br, 53bl, 53tl, 53bl, 53br, 53br, 58cla; Alain Gonfalone 39cra, 39cra.
ESTEC: 38cla.
Mary Evans Picture Library: 8tr, 8cl, 8tl, 9tl, 9tl, 9tl, 20tl, 22tl, 36tl.
CSG 1995: Genesis Space Photo Library 12bl.
Dr. Martyn Gorman, University of Aberdeen: 50c; Ronald Grant Archive/When Worlds Collide/Paramount 54clb; 2001: A Space Odyssey/MGM 55bl.
Hasbro International Inc.: 9br.
Hulton Getty: 21tr, 21bc.
Professor Kenichi Ijiri: 54cla; Image Bank 57tl.
Used with permission from McDonald's Corporation: 54l.
Matra Marconi Space UK Ltd.: 51tr; Mattels UK Ltd. 9cb.
NASA: 7tr, 7br, 10clb, 11tr, 11cr, 13clb, 15tl, 16tl, 16cl, 17cla, 17br, 17tr, 20clb, 20bc, 23tr, 30tr, 30clb, 30cr, 31tr, 32br, 32tl, 33cla, 33bl, 33tr, 34cl, 34bl, 34crb, 35cla, 35tl, 37bl, 37br, 38cr, 38crb, 38clb, 38tl, 39cb, 39cl, 40cl, 52tl, 54tr, 54cb, 56tr, 56bl, 58bc, 58ca, 58tr, 58cra; JPL 22-23, 46tr, 46c.
NASDA: 15cb.
The National Motor Museum, London: 15tc.
The Natural History Museum, London: 23cla.
Novosti (London): 18bl, 19crb,

20crb, 34tr, 34bc, 35cb, 37tl, 46crb.
Professor John Parkinson: NASA 8br, 39tl,39tc, 39tr.
Popperfoto: 15tr; Popperfoto-Reuter 21crb, 21crb, 44tl.
Rex Features: 8bl, 9cl, 9tr, 36bc, 48cl.
Science Museum: Science and Society Picture Library 15ca.
Science Photo Library: Dr. Jeremy Burgess 8cb; Robert Chase 57c; CNES, 1988 Distribution Spot Image 50-51cb; Luke Dodd 10cr; EOSAT 50tr; Will and Deni McIntyre 56tl; Larry Mulvehill 57bl; NASA 11cb, 17tl, 19bl, 34c, 44tr, 52cl, 52-53, 52br, 52bl, 59br, 59tl; Novosti 14tr, 19tr, 19tl; David Parker 48clb; Princess Margaret Rose Orthopaedic Hospital 56cb; Roger Ressmeyer, Starlight 12br.
Smith Sport Optics Inc., Idaho: 56c.
Shimizu Corporation: 54tr; Tony Morrison/South American Pictures 8cr.
Spar Aerospace (UK) Ltd.: 13tl.
Tony Stone Images: Hilarie Kavanagh 51cr; Marc Muench 11br; Charles Thatcher 56br.
Dr John Szelskey: 41tl, 44cra.
Michael Powell: Times Newspapers Ltd. 40bl.
Dean and Chapter of York: York Minster Archives 9bl.

Jacket: all DK special photography, with the exception of:
Mary Evans Picture Library: inside flap cla.
ESA: front c.
NASA: back tl; JPL back bl.

SUBJECTS

HISTORY

AFRICA

ANCIENT CHINA

ARMS & ARMOR

BATTLE

CASTLE

COWBOY

EXPLORER

KNIGHT

MEDIEVAL LIFE

MYTHOLOGY

NORTH AMERICAN INDIAN

PIRATE

PRESIDENTS

RUSSIA

SHIPWRECK

TITANIC

VIKING

WITCHES & MAGIC-MAKERS

ANCIENT WORLDS

ANCIENT EGYPT

ANCIENT GREECE

ANCIENT ROME

AZTEC, INCA & MAYA

BIBLE LANDS

MUMMY

PYRAMID

THE BEGINNINGS OF LIFE

ARCHEOLOGY

DINOSAUR

EARLY HUMANS

PREHISTORIC LIFE

THE ARTS

BOOK

COSTUME

DANCE

FILM

MUSIC

TECHNOLOGY

BOAT

CAR

FLYING MACHINE

FUTURE

INVENTION

SPACE EXPLORATION

TRAIN

PAINTING

GOYA

IMPRESSIONISM

LEONARDO & HIS TIMES

MANET

MONET

PERSPECTIVE

RENAISSANCE

VAN GOGH

WATERCOLOR

SCIENCE

ASTRONOMY

CHEMISTRY

EARTH

ECOLOGY

ELECTRICITY

ELECTRONICS

ENERGY

EVOLUTION

FORCE & MOTION

HUMAN BODY

LIFE

LIGHT

MATTER

MEDICINE

SKELETON

TECHNOLOGY

TIME & SPACE

SPORT

BASEBALL

FOOTBALL

OLYMPICS

SOCCER

SPORTS

ANIMALS

AMPHIBIAN

BIRD

BUTTERFLY & MOTH

CAT

DOG

EAGLE &
BIRDS OF PREY

ELEPHANT

FISH

GORILLA,
MONKEY & APE

HORSE

INSECT

MAMMAL

REPTILE

SHARK

WHALE

HABITATS

ARCTIC & ANTARCTIC

DESERT

JUNGLE

OCEAN

POND & RIVER

SEASHORE

THE EARTH

CRYSTAL & GEM

FOSSIL

HURRICANE &
TORNADO

PLANT

ROCKS & MINERALS

SHELL

TREE

VOLCANO &
EARTHQUAKE

WEATHER

THE WORLD
AROUND US

BUILDING

CRIME & DETECTION

FARM

FLAG

MEDIA &
COMMUNICATIONS

MONEY

RELIGION

SPY

Future updates and editions will be available online at www.dk.com

A–Z

DK EYEWITNESS BOOKS

1–110

Future updates and editions will be available online at www.dk.com

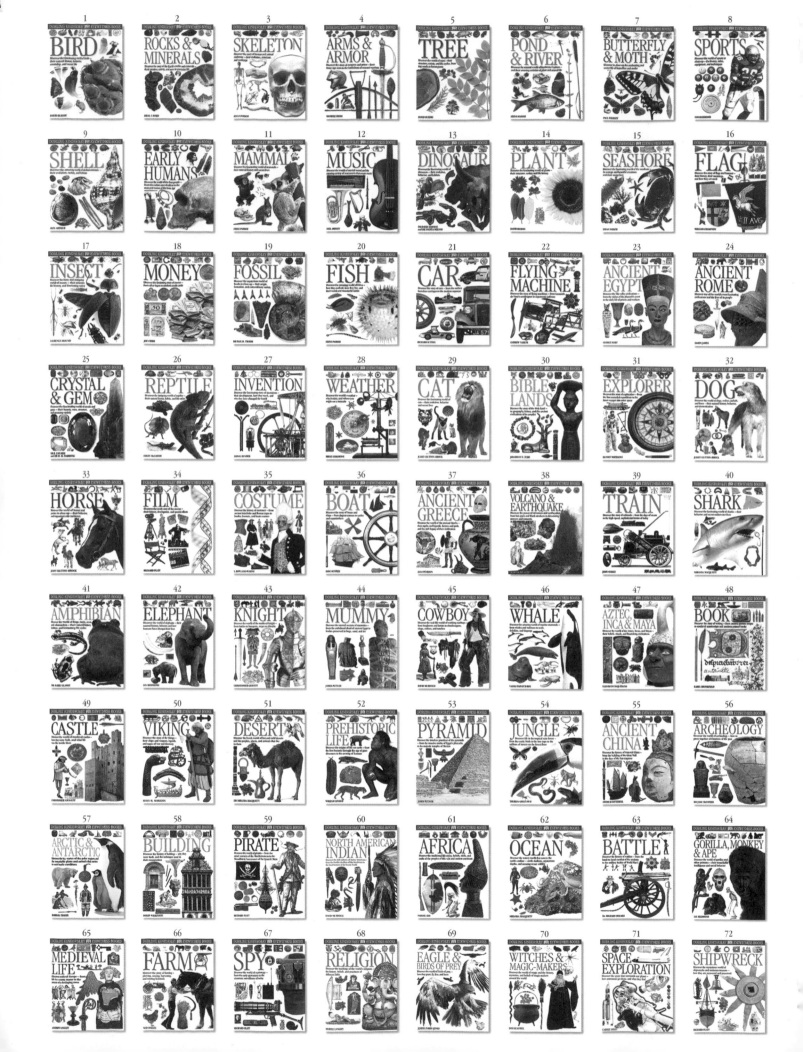

DORLING KINDERSLEY EYEWITNESS BOOKS

1	2	3	4	5	6	7	8
BIRD	ROCKS & MINERALS	SKELETON	ARMS & ARMOR	TREE	POND & RIVER	BUTTERFLY & MOTH	SPORTS

9	10	11	12	13	14	15	16
SHELL	EARLY HUMANS	MAMMAL	MUSIC	DINOSAUR	PLANT	SEASHORE	FLAG

17	18	19	20	21	22	23	24
INSECT	MONEY	FOSSIL	FISH	CAR	FLYING MACHINE	ANCIENT EGYPT	ANCIENT ROME

25	26	27	28	29	30	31	32
CRYSTAL & GEM	REPTILE	INVENTION	WEATHER	CAT	BIBLE LANDS	EXPLORER	DOG

33	34	35	36	37	38	39	40
HORSE	FILM	COSTUME	BOAT	ANCIENT GREECE	VOLCANO & EARTHQUAKE	TRAIN	SHARK

41	42	43	44	45	46	47	48
AMPHIBIAN	ELEPHANT	KNIGHT	MUMMY	COWBOY	WHALE	AZTEC, INCA & MAYA	BOOK

49	50	51	52	53	54	55	56
CASTLE	VIKING	DESERT	PREHISTORIC LIFE	PYRAMID	JUNGLE	ANCIENT CHINA	ARCHEOLOGY

57	58	59	60	61	62	63	64
ARCTIC & ANTARCTIC	BUILDING	PIRATE	NORTH AMERICAN INDIAN	AFRICA	OCEAN	BATTLE	GORILLA, MONKEY & APE

65	66	67	68	69	70	71	72
MEDIEVAL LIFE	FARM	SPY	RELIGION	EAGLE & BIRDS OF PREY	WITCHES & MAGIC-MAKERS	SPACE EXPLORATION	SHIPWRECK